Sandwiches
&Canapés

First published 2005 under the title:
"Sandwichs, tartines & canapés" by Kubik éditions
© Archipel studio, 2005

This edition © Kubik/RvR 2005
RvR Verlagsgesellschaft
Schulstr. 64
D-77694 Kehl
info@kubikinternational.de
www.kubikinternational.de

DESIGN: Thomas Brisebarre

EDITOR: Laure Desforges

COPY EDITOR: Kate van den Boogert

ISBN: 3-938265-15-9

Printed in Spain in April 2005

Constance Borde & Sheila Malovany-Chevallier

Sandwiches
&Canapés

Photography: Sophie Boussahba

Food styling: Emmanuelle Javelle

KUBIK
PUBLISHING   RvR

Con

tents

Long live the sandwich!

The sandwich has certainly come a long way since its invention in the 18th century! Contrary to most beliefs, the sandwich was not invented by the Americans, nor did it come from the Sandwich Islands. Conventional wisdom and geography aside, it was an English Lord John Montagu, Fourth Count of Sandwich, too busy at the gaming table to have a proper meal, who called for buttered bread layered with meat to be brought to him so he could eat and bet at the same time.

The sandwich has long since left the gaming table and entered our everyday lives: from home to the workplace to the hiking trail, the sandwich has become a classic way to eat or snack. And people seem to agree: if you want to eat well and quickly, the sandwich is the healthy answer.

And sandwiches have turned themselves inside out to please. Open-faced or closed, in any size you choose, hot, cold or warm, good sandwiches can be simple or sophisticated, unusual or conventional, exotic or plain. They come from all over the world, bringing us a wealth of tastes and combinations. The sandwich takes its rightful place among good foods for everyday eating, for special gourmet occasions, for picnics, buffets, cocktail parties and receptions. Try the Monte-Cristo with cheese and turkey, or the classic corned beef Reuban with cabbage and Gruyère. How about a homemade cheeseburger? Isn't it time to try a vegetarian pita (not reserved for the vegetarian alone)? Or a pepper sandwich on garlic bread?

Health food enthusiasts and dieters, gourmets and vegetarians can all savour the "new wave" sandwich. The variety and nutritional qualities, including the fibre content of breads today make bread the choice ingredient for balanced eating. Eating a delicious sandwich at the right time can do away with those middle-of-the-afternoon hunger pangs. Filled with combinations of vegetables, herbs, spices, meat, fish, or cheese, the sandwich satisfies your hunger and keeps you fit.

The esteemed place of the sandwich on menus today marks a real change. More refined, convivial and original, sandwiches now suit all occasions: buffets, cocktail parties small and large, fancy or not, and get-togethers of all kinds. Tramezzini, canapés, or open-faced sandwiches are the life of the party! Are you planning afternoon tea? Brunch or continental breakfast? Or simply drinks with friends? Try sandwiches.

The sandwich goes beyond a slice of meat or cheese between two pieces of bread. We've looked to different countries to find new versions. From Italy hails the bruschetta – toasted country-style bread rubbed with garlic, and the tramezzini – little triangles of white bread filled with tasty ingredients that Romans love to snack on mid-morning; from the Middle-East comes pita bread spread with hummus or aubergine caviar, or fresh ingredients wrapped in thin sheets of lavash; in northern Europe rye bread or pumpernickel match up tastily with salmon or smoked fish and dill.

Discover new ways to use different varieties of breads, combining them with ingredients that are new to sandwiches. Caterers and chefs have, of late, been freely reinventing the art of the sandwich by using ingredients with exotic flavours, textures and colours. And you can, too. Whether you're a consummate chef or an eager beginner, making sandwiches can be fun and creative.

Join us on this culinary adventure.
We'll give you the ideas you need to get started. Begin by tasting an open-faced canapé of sherry crab, or Époisses cheese and pears, radish and mustard seed tea sandwiches, turkey and black-bean wraps, bruschetta with lentils and foie-gras, left-over fish sandwiches with horseradish and capers, and many more.

Starting with these recipes and suggestions, you can invent other unusual combinations and audacious mixes. Spread your bread with our blue-cheese and spring onions, caponata, salsa sauce, aubergine caviar, guacamole, anchovy paste, tapenade, garlic purée, tomato and ginger chutney, pesto, apple mustard, chili ketchup, home-made pickles, courgette relish, roasted peppers, and then pile on ingredients of your choice. Worlds of new taste possibilities await you.

Bon appétit !

Constance & Sheila

Bread basket

**1. Hamburger
or sandwich buns**
Soft round hamburger
buns are made with white
flour, butter, yeast and
salt and topped
sometimes with sesame
seeds. They are
traditional for
hamburgers.

2. Brioche bread
A light egg yeast bread
with a feathery, tender
inside, similar to a brioche
but less sweet. It can
found in loaf or braided
challah form and is
especially good for grilled
vegetable or lentil and foie
gras sandwiches.

3. Hot dog rolls or buns
These soft oval yeast
rolls are highly
recommended for lobster
rolls and other salad
sandwiches, like tuna fish
or egg salad, as they
deliciously absorb some
of the tastes.

4. Rolls
Round or oval, these
individual breads are crisp
and crusty on the outside
and tender on the inside.
They can be found in
whole-wheat, rye, or white
flour. They are thus
perfect for self-contained
individual sandwiches.

5. Baguette
The characteristic French
bread, traditionally baked
in a wood-fired stone
hearth, has a crispy crust.
Inside the dough is soft
and light. The baguette
has a delightful aroma,
and is made to be eaten
right away. Long and thin,
nothing is better for the
famous and simple
"jambon-beurre".

6. White bread
Soft and tender with
a thin crust, good white
bread makes delicious
sandwiches and is
"de rigueur" for tea
sandwiches, canapés and
tramezzini. Toasted or not,
it is the base for the
renowned club sandwich.

7. Olive bread
Usually a hearty bread,
made with olive oil and
olives, and sometimes a bit
of rosemary, this is ideal
for sandwiches using
grilled peppers, pesto,
tomatoes and other
Mediterranean ingredients.

1. Rye bread

Rye flour contains very little gluten, which explains its particular flavour. Rye bread is soft yet dense and comes in round and oval shapes. Often caraway or cumin seeds are added which provide an even more distinctive flavour. Rye bread is especially popular in Germany, Russia and other northern European countries, and goes well with ham, pastrami, salami, cheese and fish; in fact, with just about anything.

2. Black bread or pumpernickel

Pumpernickel is the most famous and also the darkest of the black breads, made from coarsely ground rye wheat. It has a deliciously acid flavour and is one of an enormous variety of German breads, often steam cooked in closed moulds. Use this bread for the Nordic club sandwich, or with turkey and apple mustard, or cold or smoked fish and relish.

3. Walnut whole-wheat bread

This round or oval loaf looks great on a party platter and is delicious and tasty. The whole-wheat flour contrasts with the walnuts – and sometimes raisins are also added – providing a perfect partner for cheese, ham, smoked meat and salami.

4. Multi-grain bread

It comes in all shapes and in rolls. It is immensely popular because it is delicious and healthy with a high fibre content. The crust can be soft or crusty, but inside the multitude of cereal combinations such as millet, rye, oats, sesame, and sunflower seeds give it a crunchy texture.

5. Country-style sourdough bread

Thanks to Lionel Poilâne, France – and the world – has rediscovered this wonderful traditional bread now found on tables from Los Angeles to Hong Kong. It has a thick, crisp domed crust and its dough has a slightly acid taste. It makes wonderful slices that toast perfectly and give off an irresistible perfume. It is the perfect bread for a "meal in a sandwich", for leftover delights like meat loaf, and for bruschetta because the bread remains firm. Leaven or yeast is necessary to make bread. The former is produced from natural fermentation of the mixture of flour and water. It is kept carefully and reused for each batch of bread. Yeast is a 1-cell fungus that is used fresh or dried.

3

2

1. Ciabatta

An Italian classic popular the world over, ciabatta is a marvellous, delicately sour country bread, made with yeast, flour, milk and olive oil. The result is a crusty, tender and supple bread that comes in many forms, including rolls. It slices easily and the rolls are perfect for *pan bagnat*.

2. Pita bread

A flat, round, yeast-leavened bread baked in a very hot oven. The two layers separate during baking, creating a hollow centre. Split open, they create a pocket that can be filled to make a tasty sandwich.

3. Lavash or Armenian bread wrap

Here's a good example of the internationalisation of food products. Coming from Armenia, the Eastern Mediterranean, Iran and the Caucuses, the lavash is a traditional thin flatbread cooked directly on a stone hearth or at the back of a brick oven. It's becoming increasingly common on supermarket shelves in Europe and the USA. These round flatbreads come several sheets to a pack, and can also be found in a smaller rectangular form. Spread or layered with ingredients, they roll up easily to make rolled sandwiches or wraps that have a festive air to them.

4. Tortilla

A staple of Mexican cooking, tortillas are traditionally made with corn flour. Similar in shape to lavash, they can be spread or layered with meat, fish, vegetables and cheese and rolled into sandwiches.

5. Swedish crackers

Swedish crackers are made mainly from rye flour. They are crispy and belong on your party platter for tasty open-faced sandwiches.

6. Polar or Swedish bread

Polar bread, also called Swedish bread, is a round, soft flatbread with dimples, made with rye and wheat flour and with a slightly sweet taste. It comes from Swedish Lapland and is making its way around Europe. It makes delicious sandwiches, toasted or not, and is perfect for the Nordic club sandwich.

A Meal in a Sandwich

Egg, Anchovy and Onion ▸

For 4 sandwiches
4 rolls
2 garlic cloves, peeled
1 tbsp vinegar
2 tbsp olive oil
salt, freshly ground pepper
1 handful mesclun leaves
8 spring onions, finely sliced
1 roasted green pepper (see p. 141),
sliced lengthwise into thin strips
2 tomatoes, sliced
2 hardboiled eggs, sliced
8 anchovy fillets (fresh or canned)
16 pitted black olives
a few basil leaves

Slice open the rolls, remove some of the bread from inside, then rub the interior with the garlic cloves. Make a vinaigrette with the oil, vinegar, salt and pepper and drizzle the inside of the roll with a few drops, saving the rest for later. On the bottom half of the roll, layer some mesclun, onion slices, green pepper strips, tomato and lastly the egg slices. Top with anchovies, olives and basil leaves. Drizzle the rest of the vinaigrette over these ingredients and then close with the top half of the roll. Press together lightly, cut in half, and serve.

Salad Sandwiches

Tuna Salad

For 2 sandwiches
4 slices white or whole-wheat bread
1 can (140 g/4½ fl oz) tuna
in brine, drained
1 onion, finely chopped
1 celery stalk, finely chopped
¼ green pepper, finely minced
5 tbsp mayonnaise (see p. 138)
+ 1 tbsp for spreading
juice of ½ lemon
salt, freshly ground pepper
1 hardboiled egg,
chopped (optional)

Combine the tuna, onion, celery and green pepper in a bowl. Toss gently with a fork. Mix in the mayonnaise and lemon juice. Add salt and pepper to taste. Fold in the optional egg.

Spread the bread slices lightly with mayonnaise. Spread the tuna salad on two of the slices of bread and then cover with the other two. Slice the sandwich diagonally and serve.

This sandwich is delicious on toast, and the mayonnaise can be replaced by low-fat sour cream or yoghurt.

Fresh Tuna and Cabbage Salad

For 6 sandwiches
6 buns or 6 ciabattas
60 ml/5 tbsp Chinese mustard
(see p. 135)
FOR THE CABBAGE SALAD
¼ head white cabbage
2 garlic cloves, finely minced
1 tsp fresh ginger, finely chopped
2 tbsp lemon juice
5 tbsp oil, preferably sunflower
2 tsp sesame oil
2 tsp curry powder
2-3 drops soy sauce
FOR THE TUNA
1 tbsp oil, preferably sunflower
salt, freshly ground pepper
6 fresh tuna fillets
(approx. 40 g/1½ oz each)

Preheat the oven to 200° C/400° F/th. 6.

Prepare the cabbage: core and cut it into very thin strips, then set it aside in a bowl. In another bowl mix together the garlic, ginger and lemon juice. Drizzle the oil, the sesame oil and the curry powder in, stirring constantly with a whisk. Pour this mixture over the cabbage, mixing well, and season with the soy sauce. Set aside.

Prepare the tuna: heat the oil in a frying pan to a high temperature. Season the tuna fillets to taste then sauté them in the frying pan for about 2 minutes on each side.

Slice open the buns and place 1 tuna fillet on each one. Spread with Chinese mustard, and then add a generous portion of the cabbage mixture. Close the sandwiches and put them in the preheated oven for a few minutes until golden brown. Slice each sandwich in 2 and serve warm.

Chicken Salad

For 4 sandwiches
8 slices sourdough bread
250 g/8 oz cold cooked chicken, diced
1 small onion, chopped
1 celery stalk, chopped
2 tbsp green pepper, chopped
3 tbsp mayonnaise (see p. 138)
salt, freshly ground pepper
l hardboiled egg, chopped

In a bowl toss together the chicken, onion, celery and green pepper, and then mix in the mayonnaise. Season and fold in the egg. Spread the mixture onto 4 of the slices, and cover with the other 4. Cut the sandwiches in 2 and serve.

For a healthy variation, substitute yoghurt for the mayonnaise.

Salad Sandwiches

Chicken Breast and Homemade Pickles

For 2 sandwiches
4 slices sourdough bread, toasted
1 tsp curry
1 tbsp yoghurt
1 generous pinch of salt
1 boned chicken breast, approx.
200 g/7 oz
1 tsp oil
2 tbsp pickles, chopped
(see p. 138)
1 small onion, finely sliced
a few rocket leaves

Blend the curry and the yoghurt together, add salt, and spread on the chicken breast. Heat the oil in a frying pan over a low flame and sauté the chicken 7-8 minutes on each side. Remove, and when the chicken is room temperature, slice into thin strips. Spread the pickles on 2 slices of the toasted bread, add some onion slices, the chicken, then a few rocket leaves. Close the sandwiches with the 2 remaining slices of toast, then cut each sandwich in half to serve.

Salad Sandwiches

Coriander Crab ▸

For 3 sandwiches
6 slices sourdough bread, toasted
1 can crab meat, 165 g/5^1/$_2$ oz
grated rind and juice of 1 lime
a few drops of Tabasco sauce
salt, freshly ground pepper
2 tbsp mayonnaise (see p. 138) or
thick yoghurt
1 handful fresh coriander, coarsely
chopped
^{1}/$_2$ cucumber, thinly sliced
2 or 3 hardboiled eggs, thinly sliced
2-3 pinches paprika

Combine the crab, the lime rind, the Tabasco and the lime juice in a bowl. Toss together lightly with a fork. Add salt and pepper to taste. Spread mayonnaise on the 6 slices of toasted bread. Evenly divide the crab mixture over 3 of the slices, and layer the coriander, cucumber and half of the egg slices. Close the sandwiches with the 3 remaining slices of toast. Serve each sandwich on a plate garnished with egg slices sprinkled with paprika.

‹ Lobster Roll

For 4 sandwiches
4 hot-dog rolls
250 g/8 oz lobster meat
(1 small lobster)
100 g/3 oz celery, coarsely
chopped
1 tsp Dijon mustard
3 tbsp mayonnaise (see p. 138)
1 tbsp butter

Chop the lobster meat into $1/2$ inch (1 cm) cubes and put them in a bowl. Combine with celery, mustard and mayonnaise, and stir lightly with a fork.

Cover this preparation and let it sit for 20 minutes in the fridge.

Heat the butter in a frying pan and lightly brown the outsides of the hot-dog rolls. Open them lengthwise and fill with the lobster preparation. Serve immediately.

In the summer of 1604, French colonists settled in Maine, the most northeastern point in the United States, to trap lobster and thus gave birth to the oldest industry in the country. **LOBSTERS** are so abundant in this region that hundreds of recipes have been invented to use them, including the famous lobster roll sandwich.

Egg Salad Sandwich

For 4 sandwiches
8 slices white or whole-wheat,
toasted
4 hardboiled eggs
50 g/2 oz celery, chopped
1 tbsp chopped onion
5 tbsp mayonnaise (see p. 138)
2 tsp Dijon mustard
1 tbsp finely chopped chives

Crush the eggs with a fork and blend with the celery, onion and mayonnaise mixed with mustard. Sprinkle in the chives.
Spread all the toasted bread slices with mayonnaise on one side. Spoon the egg mixture on 4 slices and close with the 4 remaining slices, mayonnaise inside. Cut the sandwiches diagonally in 2 or 4 triangles.

You can vary this recipe by substituting yoghurt or sour cream for the mayonnaise.

Salad Sandwiches

BLT (Bacon, Lettuce and Tomato)

For 2 sandwiches
4 slices white bread
6 slices bacon
2 tbsp mayonnaise (see p. 138)
2 small tomatoes, sliced
2 large leaves iceberg lettuce

Fry the bacon in a frying pan fot approximately 3 minutes on each side, then place on a piece of paper towel to absorb the excess grease. Bacon can also be easily cooked in a microwave oven, wrapped in paper towel. For 4 slices, count about 3 minutes at maximum power.

Lightly toast the bread, and then spread 1 side with mayonnaise.

Place the tomato slices on 2 pieces of toast, then the bacon, and finally the lettuce. Close the sandwiches with the remaining slices of toast, mayonnaise inside and cut in half diagonally.

Salad Sandwiches

Chicken, Onion and Rocket ▸

For 3 sandwiches
1 baguette
1 tbsp olive oil
salt, freshly ground pepper
2 boned chicken breasts
1 onion, thinly sliced
a few rocket leaves
4 tbsp tomato chutney (see p. 132)

Heat the oil in a frying pan. Season the chicken breasts with salt and pepper, then sauté them in the oil, over medium heat, for 10-15 minutes until they are golden brown and cooked on the inside. Remove to a plate.

In the same frying pan sauté the onions for 8-10 minutes, adding a bit more oil if necessary to keep them from sticking.

Slice the chicken in fine, 1/4 inch (1/2 cm), strips.

Split the baguette in half lengthwise. On the bottom half layer the chicken strips and onions, then top with rocket leaves. Spread the top piece of bread with the tomato chutney, then close the sandwich, pressing lightly to hold it together. Cut the baguette in 3 equal pieces.

You can replace the baguette with individual ciabatta rolls.

Mozzarella, Tomato and Rocket

For 1 sandwich
2 slices white bread
1 tomato sliced
3 tsp balsamic vinegar
4 tsp olive oil
salt, freshly ground pepper
50 g/2 oz rocket
juice from 1 lemon
100 g/3½ oz mozzarella
in ½ inch (1 cm) slices

Arrange the tomato slices in a soup dish and cover them with a teaspoon of the oil, the vinegar, salt and pepper. Marinate 20 minutes.

In a bowl toss the rocket together with the rest of the oil, the lemon juice, salt and pepper.

On two slices of bread, layer the marinated tomatoes, the mozzarella and the rocket leaves. Place the other slices of bread on top, and press them down lightly. Serve sandwiches sliced diagonally in half.

You can replace the white bread with individual ciabatta rolls.

Gorgonzola and Pear

For 4 sandwiches
8 slices nut bread
180 g/6 oz Gorgonzola (or other
blue cheese: Roquefort, English
Stilton, Danish Blue,
Bleu d'Auvergne, etc.)
2 tbsp sour cream or yoghurt
2 hard pears

Using a fork, crumble the blue cheese and then mix in the sour cream. Spread this on half the bread slices. Peel and core the pears, and slice them into thin strips. Arrange them over the cheese. Close the sandwich with the remaining nut bread, and cut in half to serve.

Salad Sandwiches

Classic Club Sandwich ▸

For 1 sandwich
3 slices white bread
2 tbsp mayonnaise (see p. 138)
a few lettuce leaves
3 tomato slices
50 g/2 oz cooked chicken,
sliced finely
1 or 2 slices hard cheese
(Gruyère, Cheddar or Gouda)
1 slice ham

Toast the bread and spread one side with mayonnaise.

On one of the slices, layer the lettuce, tomato and chicken. Add another slice of bread and layer the cheese and the ham. Close the sandwich with the last slice of toast, and cut diagonally twice to obtain 4 little triangles.

Slices of hardboiled eggs can also be added, using a little less chicken (30g/1 oz).

The mayonnaise can be replaced by salad dressing (sour cream, mustard, salt and balsamic vinegar).

The **CLUB SANDWICH** is the classic of all sandwiches and it's delicious. The idea is simple: raw vegetables and chicken between three slices of white bread with mayonnaise. It started out in men's clubs where it became *de rigueur*, and the first description of this sandwich appeared in a New York magazine in the early 20th century. Now it's appreciated all over the world.

Nordic Club Sandwich

For 2 sandwiches
3 slices white bread
3 slices whole-wheat or
pumpernickel bread
1 avocado
2 tbsp lemon juice
salt, freshly ground pepper
a few sprigs of chervil, chopped
1 tbsp cream cheese
50 g/2 oz smoked salmon
(2 slices)
a few sprigs of dill, chopped
50 g/2 oz shrimp, cooked, shelled
2 lettuce leaves

Toast the bread.

Cut the avocado in half, peel and stone, then mash and sprinkle with lemon juice. Add salt and pepper and fold in the chervil.

Build the sandwiches, alternating slices of dark and white bread.

Spread the first slice with cream cheese, then add the salmon and dill. Place another bread slice of the other colour, then add the avocado purée and the shrimp. Top with a lettuce leaf, and close the sandwich. Cut in half diagonally to serve.

Salad Sandwiches

The **PAN BAGNAT**, a savoury treat from the South of France, is found on café menus, at stands on beaches, and in picnic baskets. The name means "soaked bread", as the bread (usually a round roll, but also a short loaf of French bread) is generously dribbled with olive oil and then filled with all the delicious ingredients found in a niçoise salad.

Pan bagnat

For 4 sandwiches
4 individual rolls
6 cl/2 fl oz olive oil + 1 tbsp for the peppers
2 tbsp wine vinegar
1 garlic clove, crushed
1 tsp Dijon mustard
salt, freshly ground pepper
1 red pepper, sliced, cooked and marinated in olive oil
1/4 head curly endive
2 tomatoes, sliced
8 green pepper rings, thinly sliced
1 red pepper, sliced, cooked and marinated in olive oil
12 black olives, pitted and cut in half
1 can (140 g/4 1/2 fl oz) of tuna in brine, drained
1 can/2 oz anchovy fillets, drained, cut in half lengthwise
2 hardboiled eggs, sliced
1 tbsp chopped fresh parsley
3 basil leaves

In a small bowl, make a vinaigrette dressing with olive oil, wine vinegar, garlic, and mustard. Season with salt and pepper.

Cut the bread in half lengthwise. Brush each half with the vinaigrette dressing. Arrange some endive leaves on the bottom half of the bread. Dip the tomato slices and the green peppers in the remaining vinaigrette and arrange over the endive, then add the red pepper strips. Top with tuna, eggs, anchovy, olives, chopped parsley and basil.

Wrap each piece in aluminium foil, place on a plate and weigh down with another heavy plate. Refrigerate for an hour before serving.

Salad Sandwiches

Reuben Sandwich

For 2 sandwiches
4 slices rye bread
4 tbsp mayonnaise (see p. 138)
a few drops Tabasco sauce
2 tbsp chopped celery
1 tbsp finely chopped green pepper
4 thin slices pikelfleich or
corned-beef
4 slices Gruyère
4 heaping tbsp sauerkraut
2 tbsp butter
2 dill pickles

Mix the mayonnaise, Tabasco, the celery and the green pepper together in a bowl.

On 2 of the slices of bread, layer a slice of corned beef, a slice of cheese, the sauerkraut, the celery-pepper mixture then another slice of corned beef and cheese. Close the sandwich with the 2 remaining slices of bread.

Melt half the butter in a frying pan and cook the sandwiches over a medium flame for 4-5 minutes on each side. Add more butter if necessary. Cut each sandwich in 2 and serve warm garnished with a dill pickle cut into 4 lengthwise.

The **REUBEN SANDWICH**, created in 1914 for Annette Seelos, a star from Charlie Chaplin films, is a great New York classic. It was invented by Arnold Reuben, owner of the famous delicatessen, Reuben's, once a hot spot for celebrities from the film, political and newspaper worlds.

Salad Sandwiches

Hero Sandwich

For 1 sandwich
½ baguette
1 tbsp mayonnaise (see p. 138)
and 1 tsp mustard
2-3 slices roast beef, thinly sliced
4 slices Gruyère, thinly sliced
1 tomato, sliced
a few leaves iceberg lettuce
3 slices onion, thinly sliced

Layer the ingredients on the bread, then cut the sandwich in half, thirds or quarters depending on your appetite.

Baguette

The **HERO SANDWICH** is a meal in itself: a whole loaf of French bread filled with a multitude of ingredients like ham, cheese, roast beef, salami, turkey or chicken meat, lettuce, tomatoes, pickles and more. Infinite combinations of ingredients can go into the Hero Sandwich. The meatball hero with tomato sauce is another favorite. Also known as a "grinder" or a "submarine sandwich" ("sub"), the version found in the southern United States is call a poor boy, or po'boy.

The recipe given here is classic and without frills, but feel free to add to it.

Moroccan Hero ▸

For 4 sandwiches
1 baguette
1 tbsp paprika
1 tsp cumin
1 tsp four-spice powder (cinnamon, ginger, cloves, allspice)
1 medium-sized aubergine, cubed
1 red pepper, cubed
1 yellow pepper, cubed
1 medium onion, diced
25 cl/8 fl oz water
2 garlic cloves, chopped
3 tbsp lemon juice
salt, freshly ground pepper
1 medium-sized courgette, cubed
a few basil leaves

In a heavy-bottomed saucepan, heat the spices over a medium flame, stirring often. Add the aubergine, pepper, onion, and garlic, and then the lemon juice. Add salt and pepper. Let this simmer for 5 minutes before adding the courgette.

Simmer for about 10 minutes, until the vegetables are tender and the liquid evaporates. Set aside and cool. This can be kept in the refrigerator until making the sandwich.

Slice the baguette in half lengthwise. Spread the vegetable mixture on the bottom half, arrange the basil leaves over it, and then close the sandwich with the top half. Cut the baguette into 4 equal sandwiches.

The filling can be prepared in advance then kept for 5 days in the refrigerator

Jambon-beurre ▸

For 2 or 3 sandwiches
1 fresh baguette
2 tbsp good quality butter, softened
2 or 3 slices good ham

Split open the baguette, butter it on both insides, and arrange the ham so that it fits into the baguette. Close the baguette and cut it into 2 or 3 sandwiches.

The **FRENCH JAMBON-BEURRE**, simplicity itself, is a mouth-watering treat in any language.

Ham and Brie Cheese

For 3 sandwiches
1 baguette
3 tbsp Dijon mustard
100 g/3 oz Brie, rind removed
2 slices good ham

Split open the baguette and spread the mustard on both insides. Slice the Brie in 1/4 inch (1/2 cm) pieces and press or spread it on the bottom half. Place the ham over it. Cover with the other half of the baguette, pressing down lightly on it. Cut in 3 to serve.

Baguette

‹ Vegetarian Pita

For 1 sandwich
1 pita
2 small tomatoes, peeled, seeded and cubed
1 small cucumber, cubed
2 garlic cloves, chopped
1½ tsp fresh ginger, chopped
1 tbsp olive oil
½ tbsp vinegar
salt, freshly ground pepper
black olives, pitted and halved
3 tbsp hummus (see p. 129)
a few sprigs of fresh coriander, chopped

Stir together the tomato and cucumber cubes with the garlic, ginger, oil and vinegar.

Add salt and pepper to taste.

Cut open the pita on one side using a sharp or serrated knife to make a pocket. Spread a generous layer of hummus inside and add 3 or 4 olives cut in half.

Fill the pocket with the vegetable mixture and then sprinkle with the coriander.

The **PITA** is a flat bread, traditional in Middle Eastern cuisine. It can vary slightly according to region, but it is generally a round wheat bread. Because it is baked at high temperatures, it puffs up and then flattens, forming a pocket. This allows the pita to be opened and filled with various ingredients. A good way to open a pita easily is to heat it slightly before slicing it open. Pita bread dries out quickly, but can be revived simply by moistening and heating it for a couple of minutes in the oven, wrapped in foil.

Fresh pitas can be frozen. They can then be popped directly into a warm oven for 5 minutes to thaw before being made into a sandwich.

Cobb Salad Pita

For 4 sandwiches
4 pitas or 4 whole-wheat rolls
1½ tsp mustard
1 tbsp wine vinegar
3 tbsp olive oil
salt, freshly ground pepper
2 cooked, boned chicken breasts, cubed
½ tomato, seeded and cubed
1 small avocado, peeled, stoned, and cubed
1 hardboiled egg, mashed with a fork
4 strips of bacon, cooked and crumbled
60 g/2 oz blue cheese, crumbled (Roquefort, Gorgonzola, etc.)
4 lettuce leaves

In a medium bowl, first prepare a vinaigrette with the mustard, oil and vinegar. Add salt and pepper to taste.

Add the chicken cubes, the tomato and the avocado and toss lightly. Gently add the egg, the bacon and the cheese.

Cut open each pita on one side, using a sharp or serrated knife, making a pocket. First put in 1 or 2 salad leaves and then add the chicken-vegetable-bacon mixture.

Cut the pita in half and serve.

Shrimp Salad Pita

For 2 sandwiches
120 g/4 oz shelled shrimp or
250 g/8 oz non-shelled
2 tbsp capers
grated rind of 1 lemon
1 tbsp lemon juice
1 tbsp mayonnaise (see p. 138)
or ½ tbsp mayonnaise
with ½ tbsp yoghurt
a few drops Tabasco
2 tbsp chopped dill
salt, freshly ground pepper
4 lettuce leaves
10 thin slices cucumber

Mix in a bowl the shrimp, capers, lemon rind and juice, and mayonnaise. Add the Tabasco, dill and salt and pepper.

Using a sharp or serrated knife, cut open each pita on one side to make a pocket.

First put in the salad leaves and then add the shrimp salad. Cut the pita in half, or serve whole.

Pita

Chopped Meat Pita

For 6 sandwiches

2 tbsp olive oil

1 large onion, chopped

600 g/1¼ lb lean ground lamb

3 tbsp pine nuts (optional)

1 small red or green chilli

juice of ½ lemon

1 handful parsley, chopped

1 tsp five-spice powder (cinnamon, black pepper, star anise, anise seed, cloves)

1 pinch allspice

1 pinch Cayenne pepper

salt, freshly ground pepper

lemon quarters for garnish

Heat the oil in a frying pan and sauté the onions over a medium flame. Add the meat and the optional nuts, and stir for 10-15 minutes until brown.

Add the pepper, lemon juice, parsley, spices and salt and pepper.

Using a sharp or serrated knife, cut open each pita on one side to make a pocket.

Fill the pita with the mixture then press down to spread filling evenly.

Cut the pita in quarter, to make small triangles. Serve warm with a lemon garnish.

Red Pepper, Basil and Goat's Cheese

For 3 sandwiches
6 slices of white or whole-wheat bread
1½ tsp olive oil
1 red pepper, thinly sliced
salt, freshly ground pepper
5 drops balsamic vinegar
180 g/6 oz creamy goat's cheese
a few fresh basil leaves

Heat the oil in a frying pan then sauté the red pepper strips until just tender, 8-10 minutes. They should be slightly grilled on the outside. Add the vinegar and let them cook another 30 seconds. Add salt and pepper to taste, then remove them to a dish.

Remove crusts from the bread. Spread the goat's cheese on three of the slices, then add the peppers, and top with a few basil leaves. Close the sandwiches with the remaining bread slices, pressing down lightly with your hand. Cut each sandwich in half and arrange on a plate to serve.

Cooked Vegetables

Roasted Red Pepper on Garlic Bread ▸

For 6 sandwiches
12 slices white bread or brioche, sliced thick, about ½ inch (1 cm)
3 tbsp olive oil
2 tbsp garlic purée (see p. 130)
2 roasted red peppers (see p. 141)
2 roasted yellow peppers (see p. 141)
2 tbsp basil coulis (see p. 134)
salt, freshly ground pepper
90 g/3 oz rocket leaves

Brush each slice of bread with oil and grill until golden brown. Then spread with some garlic purée. Distribute the pepper slices on half the bread slices and dribble with the basil coulis. Season with salt and pepper to taste. Top with a few rocket leaves. Close the sandwiches with the remaining slices of bread. Cut each sandwich in half on the diagonal and serve.

Goat's Cheese and Courgette

For 4 sandwiches
4 sourdough rolls
1 courgette in ½ inch (1 cm) slices
1 tbsp olive oil
salt, freshly ground pepper
120-150 g/3-4 oz log of fresh, soft
goat's cheese
1 bunch flat parsley
2-3 tbsp tapenade or anchovy paste
(optional, see p. 130)
4 lettuce leaves

Brush the courgette slices with oil and seasoned with salt and pepper. On a barbecue or in a frying pan, grill them until tender.

Roll the goat's cheese log in the parsley. Refrigerate and slice in ¼ inch (½ cm) slices.

Split open the rolls and spread the inside with a fine layer of tapenade or anchovy paste. Layer the courgette slices, then the lettuce, and lastly the cheese slices. Close the sandwich and cut in half to serve.

Sardine and Courgette

For 4 sandwiches
8 slices sourdough bread, lightly toasted or gilled
4 sardines in olive oil
$\frac{1}{2}$ courgette
1 tablespoon capers
2 tsp tapenade (see p. 130)
2 tbsp chopped sage
or celery leaves or lovage

Drain the sardines. Slice them down the middle lengthwise and remove the bones.

Cut the courgette in about 20 thin slices.

Rinse the capers in water.

Spread the tapenade on the bread. On each of 4 slices of bread place about 5 slices of courgette and 2 half sardine fillets. Sprinkle with sage, celery or lovage, and capers and cover with the remaining bread.
Cut in half and serve.

Aubergine, Ricotta and Ham

Fore 4 sandwiches
4 individual ciabatta rolls
1 small aubergine
1 garlic clove, chopped
2 tbsp olive oil
salt, freshly ground pepper
50 g/1½ oz ricotta cheese
a few drops balsamic vinegar
2 tsp chopped mint
2 tsp chopped parsley
2 tsp chopped basil
2 tsp dried, marinated
tomatoes, chopped
4 slices Parma ham
4 tomatoes, seeded and cubed
a few whole basil leaves

Preheat the oven to 200 ℃/400 ℉/th. 1-2.

Pierce the aubergine in several places with a sharp knife, then place in oven and bake until very soft, about 40 minutes. Set aside to cool, then scoop out the inside and remove to a bowl. Add the garlic to the aubergine, then the dried tomato, 1 tablespoon of the oil, salt and pepper. Mix with a fork, forming a purée.

In another bowl, mash the ricotta with a fork, then add the vinegar, the other spoonful of olive oil, the mint, parsley and basil. Correct seasoning if necessary.

Split open the rolls and layer ricotta mixture, dried tomato, ricotta, ham slices, aubergine purée, and the fresh tomatoes.

Finish by adding some whole basil leaves, close the sandwich, and cut in half to serve.

Cooked Vegetables

Hamburger Supreme

For 5 sandwiches
5 buns, lightly toasted
500 g/1 lb ground beef
1 small onion, finely chopped
1 tbsp butter
1 egg
1 tbsp chopped parsley
salt, freshly ground pepper
flour for dusting

Heat the butter in a frying pan, add the onion, and cook for about 10 minutes until transparent and soft. In a bowl, mix together the beef, onion, egg and parsley. Season with salt and pepper.

Form 5 hamburger patties, the same size as the buns, and dust lightly with flour.

Using the same frying pan, fry the hamburgers for 4-5 minutes on each side. Open the buns, and place the hamburgers on the bottom halves. Serve the hamburger accompanied with ketchup, mustard, etc.

The **HAMBURGER**, ground beef served on a bun, is a typically American recipe. As for the trimmings, anything goes. Depending on your taste, use mayonnaise, ketchup or mustard, add tomato slices, onion slices, lettuce, pickles, relish, etc. You can turn the meat patty into a gourmet delight by mixing it with cream, herbs, grated cheese, lemon juice, bread crumbs or whatever suits your fancy. In the US, one never cuts the hamburger in half or eats it with a fork and knife, in spite of the fact that it has a tendency to drip. Just use your hands, and keep a big napkin handy !

Cooked Sandwiches

Cheeseburger

For 5 cheeseburgers
5 buns, lightly toasted
500 g/1 lb ground beef
2 tbsp chopped onion
salt, freshly ground pepper
2 tbsp oil, preferably sunflower
½ tsp Worcestershire
or Tabasco sauce (optional)
2½ oz sliced cheese
(Cheddar or similar)

Mix the meat with the onion and season with salt and pepper. Add the optional Worcestershire or Tabasco sauce.

Form 5 patties. Grill or barbecue them or fry them in the oil for 5 minutes over medium heat.

Turn them over and place a slice of cheese on each one. Let them cook until the cheese melts, about 3 minutes.

Open the buns, and place the hamburgers on the bottom halves. Serve the hamburger accompanied with ketchup, mustard, etc.

You can add vary the cheeseburger by adding bacon. Cook 5 slices of bacon for 2 minutes in a frying pan until crisp. Place the bacon on top of the cheese before serving.

Salmon Burger

For 4 sandwiches
8 slices firm country-style bread
$\frac{1}{2}$ cucumber, thinly sliced
1 tsp cider vinegar
$\frac{1}{2}$ tsp sugar
1 pinch Cayenne pepper
salt, freshly ground pepper
1 egg white
1 tbsp soy sauce
$\frac{1}{2}$ tsp chopped fresh ginger
250 g/8 oz fresh salmon fillets,
skin removed, finely cubed
1 spring onion, finely chopped
1 tsp mustard seeds
1 tsp oil, sunflower or peanut
4 lettuce leaves

Mix together the cucumber slices with the vinegar, sugar and Cayenne pepper. Season with salt and pepper.

In another bowl, mix the egg white, soy sauce and ginger, then add the salmon, onion and mustard seeds. Gently toss and season if necessary with salt and pepper. With this mixture, form 4 croquettes or "salmon burgers", each the same size as the bun.

Heat the oil in a frying pan on a high flame, drop in the salmon croquettes and cook on high for about 2 minutes on each side. Lower the flame, cover the pan, and cook for another 5 minutes, turning them mid-way through.

Place a lettuce leaf on 4 slices of bread, followed by the cucumber, and then place the salmon on top. Close the sandwiches with the remaining bread slices, and serve warm.

Cayenne pepper can be used in place of chili powder.

Cooked Sandwiches

Monte Cristo

For 2 sandwiches
6 slices white bread
2 or 3 tbsp mayonnaise
(see page 138)
1 tsp Dijon mustard
4 slices Gouda, Gruyère or Comté
4 slices turkey or
4 slices ham
4 thin slices onion
1 tbsp oil, sunflower or peanut
1 tbsp butter
1 egg
15 cl/$\frac{1}{2}$ fl oz milk

For each sandwich use 3 slices of bread. Butter one side of each slice with the mustard-mayonnaise. On 4 of the slices place a slice of cheese, a slice of meat and a slice of onion. Place the remaining 2 slices of bread, mustard and mayonnaise inside, on 2 of the 4 piles. Assemble the sandwiches by placing the bigger piles on the smaller ones, thus obtaining 2 triple-layer sandwiches. Remove the crust with a sharp knife. Wrap each sandwich tightly in plastic film and refrigerate for at least 30 minutes, but no more than 6 hours.

Heat the butter in a frying pan. During this time, beat the milk and egg with a whisk in a bowl, remove the sandwiches from the plastic film, dip them gently and evenly in the egg mixture, then brown them evenly on both sides in the frying pan, about 5 minutes, adding more butter if necessary. Cut each sandwich in 2 triangles, and serve warm.

Sloppy Joe

For 6 sandwiches
6 buns or 1 baguette, cut in 6
1 tbsp oil, sunflower or peanut
1 onion, chopped
1 small pepper, red or yellow, diced
4 garlic cloves, finely chopped
1 celery stalk, chopped
1 tsp thyme
salt, freshly ground pepper
500 g/1 lb ground beef
1 400 g/14 oz can plum
tomatoes, chopped
7 cl/2$\frac{1}{2}$ fl oz cider vinegar
1 tbsp Worcestershire sauce
12 cl/4 fl oz beer
3 tbsp chopped chives

Heat the oil in a frying pan over a medium flame. Add the onion, pepper, garlic, celery and thyme. Add salt and pepper, then lower the flame and leave to cook for 10 minutes. Don't let it burn, the onion should become transparent but not brown. Transfer to a shallow bowl and set aside.

In the same frying pan, over a medium flame, brown the meat for 10 minutes. Add the cooked vegetables, tomatoes, vinegar, Worcestershire sauce and the beer. Simmer for at least 15 minutes, partially covered, until the mixture thickens.

Toast or grill the bread cut in 2 lengthways, and then scoop 2 heaping spoonfuls on the bottom of each bun (or baguette). Sprinkle with chives, and close the sandwich. Serve warm. Unlike a hamburger, this sandwich should be eaten with a knife and fork.

Grilled Cheese Sandwich

For 2 sandwiches
4 slices white bread
75 g/2½ oz softened butter
100 g/3 oz grated cheese

Spread both sides of the bread slices with 50 g (1¾ oz) of the butter, then place cheese on 2 of the slices. Close the sandwiches with the 2 remaining slices.

Melt the butter in a large frying pan, then fry the sandwiches for 4 minutes on each side.

To make your sandwiches even better, squash them while they are cooking: spread a piece of tin foil over the sandwiches in the pan, and place a 500 g (1 lb) weight on them (a can of tomatoes, for example). Brown them on one side, then remove the weight and the foil, turn the sandwiches over, and weigh them down again.

Cooked Sandwiches

Pork in Barbecue Sauce

For 6 sandwiches

6 ciabatta rolls

RED ONION AND CUCUMBER MARINADE:

$1/2$ red onion, peeled and chopped

$1/4$ cucumber, peeled, seeded and diced

salt, freshly ground pepper

2 tbsp sunflower oil

1 tbsp wine vinegar

FOR THE MEAT:

1 tsp finely chopped garlic

1 tsp paprika

$1/2$ tsp coarse salt

$1/2$ tsp cracked pepper

500 g/1 lb pork fillet

1 tbsp sunflower oil

3 tbsp cider vinegar

2 tsp lemon juice

$1/2$ tsp red pepper flakes

FOR THE BARBECUE SAUCE:

1 tsp sunflower oil

2 tsp finely chopped shallots

1 tsp finely chopped garlic

freshly ground pepper

1 tsp cumin powder

$1/2$ tsp chile powder

$1/2$ tsp red pepper flakes

7 cl/2 oz beer

1 tbsp molasses

1 tsp tomato paste

1 tsp wine vinegar

pinch coarse salt

Prepare the marinade: toss the onion and cucumber together in a bowl. Add salt and pepper and cover with the oil and vinegar. Leave this preparation in a cool place for at least 20 minutes. Prepare the meat: mix together the garlic, paprika, coarse salt, pepper then spread over the meat. Heat the oil in a heavy-bottomed saucepan and sauté the meat. When it is brown on all sides, add the vinegar, lemon and pepper flakes. Let simmer for 30 minutes.

During this time, prepare the barbecue sauce: heat the oil in a heavy-bottomed saucepan, then add the shallots, garlic, pepper, cumin and the chili powder. Let simmer for 2 minutes. Add the pepper flakes, beer, molasses, tomato paste, wine vinegar and salt. Lower the flame and simmer this thick sauce for 10 minutes.

Prepare the sandwiches: cut the hot meat into thin slices then dip them in the barbecue sauce. Slice open the ciabatta rolls and heat or toast them. Place the meat slices dipped in barbecue sauce on the bottom half and top with the cucumber and onion marinade. Close the sandwiches, cut in half and serve warm.

In the southern United States, the influence of slaves from Africa, passing through the Carribean, and property-owners from different parts of Europe combine to produce plantation cooking. **BARBECUE SAUCE** is a key element in this spicy and colourful cuisine, and is typically American.

Cooked Sandwiches

Croque-monsieur

For 4 sandwiches
8 slices white bread
2 slices lean ham
8 slices Gruyère
50 g/1½ oz butter
freshly ground pepper
ground nutmeg

Preheat the oven to 200 °C/400 °F/th. 6-7.

Cut the ham and cheese slices to the same shape and size as the bread slices. Butter the bread slices on both sides.

Place a slice each of ham and Gruyère on 4 of the bread slices. Season with pepper and a twist of nutmeg, and then cover with the 4 remaining bread slices. Place the sandwiches on an oven shelf and bake 8 minutes on one side, and 5 minutes on the other.

Serve the croque-monsieurs hot, accompanied by a green salad.

Croque-monsieurs can also be made in a buttered frying pan. Fry over a medium flame for 5 minutes each side.

Cooked Sandwiches

Croque-monsieur and Scrambled Eggs

For 4 sandwiches
8 slices white bread
100 g/3½ oz butter
10 cl/3½ fl oz milk
4 slices ham
8 slices Gruyère
3 eggs
salt, freshly ground pepper
a little chopped parsley

Cut the ham and cheese slices to the same shape and size as the bread slices. Butter each bread slice on one side.

Layer ham then Gruyère on 4 slices of bread. Cover with the other 4 slices, butter inside.

Scramble the eggs in 25 g (1 oz) of butter in a frying pan. Add salt and pepper to taste. When they are almost cooked, add the milk and stir. Keep the eggs warm, over a saucepan of boiling water.

Melt the rest of the butter in another frying pan, then fry the sandwiches until they are golden brown on each side, about 10 minutes.

Just before serving, spoon the hot scrambled eggs over the sandwiches and sprinkle with parsley.

Croque-madame

For 4 sandwiches
8 slices white bread
8 slices Gruyère
4 slices lean ham
40 g/1½ oz butter + 10 g/½ oz for
frying the eggs
4 eggs
salt, freshly ground pepper

Preheat the oven to 200 °C/400 °F/th. 6.

Cut the ham and cheese slices to the same shape and size as the bread slices. Butter each bread slice on one side.

Layer cheese, ham then cheese on 4 slices of bread. Close with the other 4 slices, butter inside. Brown them in the oven, 8 minutes on one side, 5 minutes on the other.

During this time, fry the eggs in the remaining butter, season with salt and pepper. Remove the sandwiches from the oven and top each one with a fried egg before serving.

You can replace the Gruyère with thinly sliced goat's cheese. You can also incorporate some tomato and onion slices in the sandwich, after the ham layer.

Welsh Rarebit ▸

For 2 rarebits
2 slices white bread
2 tbsp butter
2 thick slices Cheddar cheese
2 tbsp Dijon mustard
freshly ground pepper

Preheat the over to 180 °C/350 °F/th. 4.

Using a sharp knife, remove the crusts from the bread. Toast the bread lightly golden and then spread a little butter on one side of each slice. Place each piece of toast in a small ovenproof dish, and top with a slice of cheese. Spread the mustard over the cheese. Add pepper to taste.

Cook in the oven for 7 minutes, until the cheese is completely melted. Serve the rarebits directly in the dish they are cooked in. Rarebits are not really finger sandwiches and should be eaten with a knife and fork.

The origin of **WELSH RAREBIT**, also known as Welsh rabbit, is as mysterious as its name. No one seems to agree on what the name means, but it's certain that it is not Welsh, and certainly not rabbit ! This recipe, for which there are multitudes of variations, was adapted from one by Isabella Beeton, first published in 1861 in *The Book of Household Management*.

Scotch Rarebit

For 2 rarebits
2 slices white bread
2 thick slices Cheddar cheese
2 tbsp Port
2 tbsp Dijon mustard
freshly ground pepper

Preheat the oven to 180 °C/350 °F/th. 4.

Slowly melt the cheese together with the Port in a saucepan. Add the mustard and pepper. You can also use a microwave on high for 1 minute. Spread the mixture on the toasted bread heat in the oven, in an ovenproof dish. Serve piping hot.

You can replace the Port with beer.

Cooked Sandwiches

Snack and Party Sandwiches

Ham, Gruyère and Mustard Tramezzini

For 6 tramezzini
9 slices white bread
1 tbsp softened butter
2 tsp Dijon mustard
3 thin slices ham
6 slices Gruyère cheese

Remove the crust from the bread.

Butter 3 slices of bread and spread mustard on the other 3 slices.

Cut the ham to the same shape as the bread and place a slice on the buttered bread.

Cover with the 3 plain slices of bread. Place a slice of cheese on those slices. Cover with the mustard slices, mustard on the inside.

Press the sandwiches lightly to close them and cut diagonally to form 6 neat triangles. Serve immediately.

TRAMEZZINI, these small pretty triangles, come from Italy. Made with 2 or 3 slices of soft, white, crustless bread and delicate layers of ingredients, these delicious snacks are as perfect for a mid-morning or mid-afternoon snack as for a cocktail party.

Mozzarella, Proscuitto and Pesto Tramezzini ▸

For 6 tramezzini
9 slices white bread
6 tbsp pesto (see p. 134)
6 thin slices mozzarella
3 slices prosciutto
100 g/3 oz chopped black olives

Remove the crust from the bread and spread the slices with pesto.

Distribute the mozzarella on 3 slices of bread.

Cover with the other 3 slices and layer them with a slice of ham and olives.

Cover with the remaining bread. Press the sandwiches lightly to close them and cut diagonally to form 6 near triangles. Serve immediately.

Tramezzini

Tuna, Artichoke and Garlic Tramezzini

For 6 tramezzini
9 slices white bread
90 g/3 oz canned tuna
in brine, drained
2 tbsp garlic purée (see p. 130)
salt, freshly ground pepper
3 artichoke hearts, cut in strips
2 hardboiled eggs, thinly sliced

Mash the tuna with a fork and blend in 1 tablespoon of the garlic purée.

Remove the crust from the bread. On 1 slice, spread a thin layer of the tuna mixture and then the strips of artichoke. Season with salt and pepper.

Cover with a second slice of bread that has been spread with some of the rest of the garlic purée. Place eggs slices on that slice of bread. Close the sandwich with the third slice of bread. Repeat the operation twice more. Press the sandwiches lightly to close and cut diagonally to form 6 neat triangles.

Tuna Tramezzini

For 4 tramezzini
6 slices white bread
3 small anchovies
45 g/1½ oz canned tuna
in brine, drained
30 g/1 oz softened butter or thick
yoghurt
1 tbsp capers
1 tbsp tapenade (see p. 130)

In a food processor, reduce the anchovies to a paste.

Remove the crust from the bread.

Mash the tuna with a fork while incorporating the butter and capers.

Spread 2 slices of the bread with the anchovy paste and then the tapenade. Cover them with 2 other slices of bread on which you have spread the tuna-butter-caper mixture.

Close the 2 sandwiches with the 2 remaining slices and cut them on the diagonal to form 4 neat triangles. Serve immediately.

Tramezzini

‹ Salmon, Cucumber and Dill Tramezzini

For 6 tramezzini
9 slices of white bread
50 g/1½ oz mascarpone
50 g/1½ oz cream cheese
1 tbsp chopped dill
salt, freshly ground pepper
1 cucumber, peeled
and sliced finely
3 slices smoked salmon
2 hardboiled eggs, sliced finely

Prepare a dill cream by mixing the mascarpone, the cream cheese and the dill together. Season with salt and pepper.

Remove the crust from the bread and spread the slices with dill cream.

On 3 of the slices, layer a few of the cucumber slices.

Cover each of them with a slice of smoked salmon and then a slice of bread with the dill cream on the inside.

Spread a new layer of dill cream on these slices and top with a few slices of egg. Close the sandwiches with the 3 remaining slices of bread, cream on the inside.

Cut each sandwich on the diagonal to form 6 regular triangles. Serve immediately.

Herbs and Ricotta Tramezzini

For 4 tramezzini
6 slices of white bread
100 g/3½ oz drained ricotta
1 tbsp grated Parmesan cheese
1½ tbsp olive oil
1 handful parsley
1 handful chervil
1 handful tarragon
1 handful oregano
2 spring onions, thinly sliced
5 Provençal olives,
pitted and chopped
1 tsp rice vinegar
2 tsp Dijon mustard
salt, freshly ground pepper

Mix the ricotta and the Parmesan together, adding half the oil.

Chop the herbs. Prepare a vinaigrette dressing with the rice vinegar, the rest of the oil, the mustard, salt and pepper. Add the herbs, the onion, and the olives.

Spread 2 slices of bread with the cheese mixture. Cover with 2 other slices on which you have spread the herb salad. Close the 2 sandwiches with the remaining slices of bread.

Cut each sandwich on the diagonal to form 4 neat triangles. Serve immediately.

Tramezzini

Avocado and Bacon Tramezzini

For 12 tramezzini
6 slices whole-wheat or white bread
125 g/4 oz smoked bacon
1 ripe avocado
1 grated lemon rind
1 tbsp lemon juice
salt, freshly ground pepper
30 g/1 oz softened butter

Wrap the bacon in paper towels and cook in several batches for
2-4 minutes in a microwave oven at maximum power, until crisp. Crumble
the bacon and set aside.

Peel and stone the avocado and mash with a fork, adding the lemon juice
and the grated rind. Season with salt and pepper.

Butter the bread from which you've removed the crust and spread
3 slices with the avocado purée. Sprinkle some bacon pieces on top
of those slices.

Cover with the remaining slices of bread and press down lightly.
Cut each sandwich on the diagonal to form 12 neat triangles.
Serve immediately.

You can make this recipe with olive bread and you can replace the
bacon with pancetta.

Tramezzini

Watercress and Cucumber ▸

For 8 tea sandwiches
8 thin slices white bread
100 g/3 oz cream cheese
30-40 g/1-1½ oz butter
½ cucumber, peeled
and thinly sliced
½ bunch chopped watercress
juice of ½ lemon

Spread cream cheese on 4 slices of bread and butter on the other 4.

Mix the watercress with the lemon juice.

On the cream cheese side, place the cucumber and a layer
of watercress.

Close the sandwiches with the buttered bread on the inside. Remove the
crust and cut the sandwiches on the diagonal to get 8 neat triangles or
twice diagonally for 16 smaller sandwiches. Serve immediately.

The British love **TEA SANDWICHES** – little sandwiches served at tea time. On the other side of the English
Channel, for cocktail parties, the French love their champagne with **CANAPÉS** – delicious little open-
faced sandwiches, sometimes toasted and sometimes not. It's the English version that's presented
here, but nothing stops you from removing the top slice of bread for the French canapé!

Cream Cheese and Chutney

For 8 tea sandwiches
8 thin slices white bread
100 g/3 oz cream cheese
2-3 tbsp tomato chutney
(see p. 132)
a few watercress leaves

Spread the cream cheese on 4 slices of bread, then add a layer of
chutney and a few watercress leaves.

Close the sandwiches with the other 4 slices of bread. Remove the crust
and cut the sandwiches on the diagonal to get 8 neat triangles. Serve
immediately.

Tea Sandwiches

Mint Turnip

For 24 tea sandwiches
12 thin slices white bread
3 tbsp mayonnaise (see p. 138)
3 tbsp cream cheese
1 tbsp grated lemon rind
1 tbsp lemon juice
1 tbsp wholegrain mustard
½ tsp salt
freshly ground pepper
2-3 young raw turnips
3 tbsp fresh mint leaves

Mix together the mayonnaise, cheese, lemon juice and rind, and mustard, then season with salt and pepper. Taste and if necessary, add more lemon and/or mustard.

Slice the turnips as thinly as possible.

Spread each slice of bread with the mayonnaise mixture. On 6 of the slices, put a thin layer of chopped mint and turnip slices.

Close the sandwiches with the remaining slices of bread. Remove the crust and cut the sandwiches twice diagonally to get 24 small triangles.

Enclose them in cling wrap and keep in refrigerator until ready to serve.

Radish and Mustard Seed

For 20 tea sandwiches
10 thin slices white bread
200 g/6¹/₂ oz radishes, chopped
1¹/₂ tsp mustard seed
250 g/8 oz cream cheese
1¹/₂ tsp salt
freshly ground pepper
3-4 tbsp butter, softened
a few rocket leaves

Mix together the radishes, mustard seed, cheese and salt and pepper.

Butter each slice of bread and distribute the radish mixture on 5 of them. Add the rocket leaves and close the sandwiches with the remaining slices of bread, butter on the inside.

Remove the crust and cut the sandwiches twice diagonally to get 20 neat triangles. Serve immediately.

You can replace the mustard seeds with poppy seeds and use spinach or lettuce leaves instead of rocket.

Tea Sandwiches

Aubergine Purée and White Beans

For 24 tea sandwiches
12 thin slices white bread
1 medium aubergine
5 tsp olive oil
1 garlic clove
100 g/3 oz cooked white beans
½ tbsp tahina (sesame cream)
1 tsp ground cumin
salt, freshly ground pepper
juice of 1 lemon
1 tbsp chopped flat parsley
1 tbsp chopped fresh mint

Preheat the oven to 180 °C/350 °F/th. 4.

Cut the aubergine in half lengthwise and cook for 20-25 minutes, or 7 minutes in a microwave oven at maximum power, until the skin is black and the flesh tender.

In a frying pan, heat ½ tablespoon oil over a low flame and cook the garlic until soft.

Scoop out the aubergine flesh, leaving the skin, and purée it in a food processor with the beans, garlic, the rest of the oil, the tahina, cumin, salt, pepper and lemon juice until you have a smooth and homogenous paste. Adjust the seasoning, adding more salt or pepper if necessary.

Spread a layer of this mixture on 6 of the slices of bread and then sprinkle them with the herbs. Cover with the remaining bread. Remove the crust and cut the sandwiches twice diagonally to get 24 neat triangles. Serve immediately.

Fresh Vegetables ▸

For 16 tea sandwiches
8 thin slices white bread
100 g/3 oz cream cheese
4 tbsp herbs (basil, tarragon, flat parsley, coriander) chopped and mixed together
½ cucumber, thinly sliced
6-8 radishes, thinly sliced

Spread the cream cheese on 4 slices of bread. Layer each of them with herbs, cucumber slices and radish slices. Close them with the remaining slices. Remove the crust and cut the sandwiches twice diagonally to get 16 neat triangles. Serve immediately.

Tea Sandwiches

Tuna and Tapenade

For 16 tea sandwiches
8 thin slices white bread
180 g/6 oz canned tuna
in brine, drained
2 tbsp mayonnaise (see p. 138)
4 tbsp tapenade (see p. 130)

Mash the tuna with a fork and fold in the mayonnaise.

Spread 4 slices of bread with the tuna mixture and the other 4 slices with the tapenade. Close the sandwiches with the tapenade slices, tapenade inside.

Remove the crust and cut the sandwiches twice diagonally to get 16 neat triangles. Serve immediately.

‹Salmon and Capers

For 16 tea sandwiches
8 thin slices white bread
4 tbsp cream cheese
2 capers, coarsely chopped
2 slices smoked salmon, cut in half
freshly ground pepper

Spread the cheese on 4 slices of the bread. Distribute the capers and salmon and season with pepper.

Close the sandwiches with the other 4 slices. Remove the crust and cut them twice diagonally to get 16 neat triangles. Serve immediately.

Smoked Trout Mousse

For 16 tea sandwiches
8 thin slices white bread
2 medium smoked trout
50 g/1½ oz softened butter
6 tbsp double cream
juice of 1 or 2 lemons
salt, freshly ground pepper

Skin and fillet the trout. Mash the fish with a fork and fold in the butter and cream. Mix well to obtain a purée. Add the lemon juice and season with salt and pepper.

Spread 4 slices of the bread with this mixture and close the sandwiches with the other slices.

Remove the crust and cut the sandwiches twice diagonally to get 16 neat triangles. Serve immediately.

Tea Sandwiches

Bacon and Parsley

For 32 small sandwiches
(prepare a few hours in advance)
8 thin slices of white bread
125 g/4 oz bacon or pancetta,
thinly sliced
5 tbsp chopped parsley
4 tbsp mayonnaise (see p. 138)
1/2 tsp Worcestershire sauce
1 garlic clove
1 tbsp softened butter

Wrap the bacon in paper towels and cook in several batches in a microwave oven at maximum power, until crisp.

In a food processor, mix the parsley, bacon, mayonnaise and Worcestershire sauce. Set aside.

Chop the garlic finely and fold it into the butter.

Flatten each slice of bread with a rolling pin and spread with the butter-garlic mixture. Layer that with a tablespoon of the parsley-bacon mixture.

Remove the crust from the bread. Roll the flattened slice of bread carefully to form little logs, and wrap each one in cling wrap so they keep their shape. Put them in the refrigerator. You can also keep them in the freezer for a few days; they defrost very quickly.

Before serving, remove the cling wrap and cut each log in 4 pieces.

Rolled Sandwiches

Ham, Pecorino and Tomato ▸

**For 2 rolled sandwiches or wraps
or 6 sandwich bites**
1 lavash
5 tsp mayonnaise (see p. 138)
2 slices ham
50 g/2 oz pecorino cheese, thinly
sliced
3 tomato slices
1 small handful rocket

Spread the lavash or wrap with mayonnaise. Layer the ham, cheese, tomato and rocket on the lavash or wrap, leaving 1/2 inch (1 cm) border all around. Roll tightly, tucking in the sides as you go, making a neat package. Wrap in cling film and keep in the refrigerator until ready to serve. Cut into 2 or into 6 on an angle.

Turkey and Black Bean Sauce

**For 8 rolled sandwiches or wraps
or 24 sandwich bites**
(can be prepared a few hours
in advance)
4 lavash
1 can 170 g/5½ oz fermented black
beans, drained and rinsed
1 large chopped tomato
2 jalapeño peppers, chopped
juice of 1 lime
1 tsp chili powder
1 ripe avocado, peeled and stoned
2 tbsp yoghurt
salt, freshly ground pepper
250 g/8 oz turkey breast,
thinly sliced
150 g/5 oz chopped coriander

Prepare the black bean sauce: in a bowl mix together the beans, tomato, peppers, chili and half the lime juice.

Prepare the avocado purée: in a food processor, blend the avocado with the rest of the lime juice and the yoghurt. Season with salt and pepper.

Spread a thick layer of avocado purée on the lavash sheets. Layer half the sheet with slices of turkey. Cover with 2 tablespoons of the black bean sauce and sprinkle a generous portion of coriander on top.

Roll the lavash. Cut each one on an angle to get 8 wraps. Or cut each log into 6 bites for 24 sandwich bites.

Soft tortillas can also be used instead of the lavash. Roast pork can be sliced and used instead of the turkey.

Turkey and Gruyère

**For 2 rolled sandwiches or wraps
or 6 sandwich bites**
1 lavash
1 tbsp wholegrain mustard
50 g/2 oz turkey breast,
cut in thin strips
50 g/2 oz Gruyère, thinly sliced
3 tomato slices
2 lettuce leaves

Spread the lavash with mustard. On half of the sheet, distribute the slices of turkey, cheese, tomato and lettuce leaves.

Roll the lavash with the preparation inside. Cut the wrap in 6 sandwich bites or in half on an angle before serving.

Rolled Sandwiches

Bacon, Tomato and Guacamole

For 24 sandwich bites
4 lavash
3 tomatoes
1 tbsp olive oil
8 slices bacon
8 tbsp guacamole (see p. 129)
a few lettuce leaves

Preheat the grill. Cut the tomatoes in thick slices, sprinkle olive oil on them and grill for 5-7 minutes.

Fry the bacon over a moderate flame for 3 minutes on each side; it should not be too crisp. Break each slice into 2 or 3 pieces.

Spread the guacamole generously on half of each wrap. Cover with the tomatoes, the bacon and the lettuce.

Roll up the lavash and cut each one into 6, on an angle, to get 24 pieces.

Salmon, Cucumber and Capers ▸

For 2 rolled sandwiches or wraps or 6 sandwich bites
1 lavash
$1/2$ tbsp softened butter
2 slices smoked salmon, cut in small pieces
$1/2$ cucumber, thinly sliced
1 tbsp capers
1 tbsp chopped dill
freshly ground pepper

Moisten the lavash lightly and warm it for 1-2 minutes in a traditional oven or for a few seconds in a microwave oven.

Butter the whole wrap; distribute the salmon and the cucumber over half the wrap. Sprinkle the capers and the dill over that. Season with pepper.

Roll the wrap and cut it in half on an angle or into 6 pieces.

Rolled Sandwiches

Bruschetta and Open-faced Sandwiches

Bruschetta

For 2 bruschetta
1 slice of country-style (or
sourdough) bread, ½ inch (1 cm)
thick
1 garlic clove, peeled
2 tsp olive oil
salt, freshly ground pepper

Grill or toast the bread. Rub the garlic over it and then brush it with olive oil. Season with salt and pepper. Cut it into two before serving.

In Italy, grilled or toasted slices of bread are called **BRUSCHETTAS**. In their simplest state, the bread is rubbed with garlic and brushed with olive oil. Classic versions use tomato, herbs and cheese. The bread has to be of the highest quality whether you use country-style bread, sourdough bread or even baguette. Grilling it over an open fire makes it even tastier.

The number of portions vary according to the type, form and cut of the bread used.

Classic Tomato Bruschetta ▸

For 4 bruschetta
2 slices country-style bread
2 garlic cloves, peeled
3-4 tsp olive oil
salt, freshly ground pepper
1 tomato, peeled, seeded and cubed
a few pinches oregano or basil

Grill or toast the bread. Rub the garlic over it and then brush with olive oil. Spread a few teaspoonfuls of tomato on the bread. Sprinkle with herbs and season with salt and pepper. Cut into 2 before serving.

Bruschetta

Tomato and White Bean Bruschetta

For 8 bruschetta
4 thick slices country-style bread
500 cherry tomatoes
1 garlic clove, chopped
425 g/13 oz/1 lb can white
cannelloni beans, drained
salt, freshly ground pepper
4-5 tbsp olive oil
1 tbsp red wine vinegar
2-3 garlic cloves, peeled
8 anchovies

Preheat the oven to 225° C/425 °F/th. 7.

Prick the tomatoes with a knife and mix with the chopped garlic. Season with salt and pepper and bake for 15 minutes.

Season the beans with salt and pepper and add 2 tablespoons of the oil and the vinegar. Incorporate the tomatoes, draining off any juice if necessary.

Grill or toast the bread. Rub the garlic over it and then brush with olive oil. Cut each slice of bread in half to get 8 bruschetta. Spread the preparation on the grilled bread and top with a small anchovy before serving.

‹ Mushroom and Ham Bruschetta

For 8 bruschetta
4 slices country-style bread,
½ inch (1 cm) thick
4 tbsp olive oil
250 g/8 oz cèpes (or porcini)
salt, freshly ground pepper
2-3 garlic cloves, peeled
4 thin slices Parma ham
or prosciutto
a few slivers Parmesan cheese

Clean and chop the mushrooms. Sauté them in 2 tablespoons of oil for a few minutes. Season with salt and pepper.

Grill or toast the bread on both sides until golden.

Rub the garlic over one side of the bread, and brush with the rest of the oil.

On each slice, layer the mushrooms, ham and Parmesan.

Put in the oven or under the grill to melt the cheese slightly.

Cut each bruschetta in half and serve.

Bruschetta

Roasted Courgette Bruschetta

For 8 bruschetta
4 slices country-style bread
4 tbsp olive oil
1 tbsp balsamic vinegar
4-5 garlic cloves
1 tbsp pine nuts
2 medium courgettes, cut on an
angle, ½ inch (1 cm) thick
salt, freshly ground pepper
8 basil leaves

In the food processor, mix together 2 tablespoons of the oil, the vinegar, 2 garlic cloves and the pine nuts. Spead over the courgettes and leave to marinate for 5 minutes.

Season the preparation with salt and pepper and grill it (or sauté it gently in a frying pan) until the courgettes are cooked.

Grill or toast the bread. Rub the garlic over one side of the bread, then brush with the rest of the oil.

Distribute the grilled courgettes on the bread. Cut each bruschetta in half and decorate with a basil leaf. Serve immediately.

Asparagus and Prosciutto Bruschetta

For 8 bruschetta
4 slices country-style bread
250 g/8 oz green asparagus
salt, freshly ground pepper
4 tbsp olive oil
1 tbsp wine vinegar
2-3 garlic cloves, peeled
a few rocket leaves
4 slices prosciutto

Cover the asparagus with water and cook in a saucepan until tender, about 15 minutes. While still warm, season with salt, pepper, half the oil and the vinegar.

Grill or toast the bread. Rub the garlic over one side of the bread, then brush with the rest of the oil.

On each slice of bread, layer the rocket, asparagus, and a slice of ham cut to the size of the bread. Cut each bruschetta in half and serve lukewarm.

Bruschetta

Aubergine Bruschetta

For 8 bruschetta
4 slices country-style bread
1 aubergine (500 g/1 lb)
$1/2$ tbsp coarse salt
8 anchovy fillets
2 tbsp capers
2 tbsp parsley
$1/2$ tbsp lemon juice
2 tbsp olive oil
2-3 garlic cloves, peeled
salt, freshly ground pepper
225 g/7 oz buffalo mozzarella,
thinly sliced

Cut the unpeeled aubergine into $1/2$ inch (1 cm) thick slices.

Sprinkle them with the coarse salt and let them drain for at least 1 hour. Then dry with paper towels.

In a food processor, mix together the anchovies, capers, parsley, and lemon juice to get a purée.

Brush the aubergine slices lightly with half the oil before grilling them for 3-4 minutes on each side, or until the flesh is tender.

Grill or toast the bread. Rub the garlic over one side of the bread, and then brush with the rest of the oil.

Sheep's Milk Cheese and Black Olive Bruschetta ▸

For 12 bruschetta
6 slices country-style bread
3-4 garlic cloves, peeled
6 tbsp olive oil
salt, freshly ground pepper
1 red or yellow pepper, or $1/2$ of
each, roasted (see p. 141)
2 tbsp black Provençal olives,
coarsely chopped
200 g/$6^1/2$ oz sheep's milk cheese
2 tbsp chopped parsley
2 tbsp chopped chives
2 tbsp fresh thyme or savoury

Grill or toast the bread. Rub the garlic over one side of the bread, and brush with the oil. Season with salt and pepper.

Cut the roasted pepper into cubes.

With a fork or wooden spoon, mix the cheese and the other ingredients together to obtain a smooth cream. Season with salt and pepper.

Spread this cream on the bread. Cut each slice in half and serve immediately.

Bruschetta

Mozzarella, Garlic and Greens Bruschetta

For 8 bruschetta
4 slices country-style bread
2-3 whole garlic cloves, peeled
4 tbsp olive oil
250 g/8 oz rocket or spinach
3 cloves garlic, chopped
$^{1}/_{2}$ tsp coarse salt
200 g/6$^{1}/_{2}$ oz mozzarella, cubed
freshly ground pepper

Grill or toast the bread. Rub the garlic over one side of the bread, then brush with half the oil.

Remove the hard stems of the rocket or spinach and chop the leaves coarsely. In a frying pan with the rest of the oil, cook the chopped garlic and the salt over a low flame for 5 minutes. Incorporate the rocket or spinach gently and cook for 3 minutes.

Drain off the liquid and transfer the greens to a bowl. When cool, add the mozzarella.

Spread a generous layer over each prepared slice of bread. Season with pepper and cut in half before serving.

Tomato and Ricotta Bruschetta

For 8 bruschetta
4 slices country-style bread
2-3 garlic cloves, peeled
5-6 tbsp olive oil
salt, freshly ground pepper
1 tsp balsamic vinegar
3 tomatoes, peeled, seeded
and cubed
150 g/5 oz ricotta
a few basil leaves, chopped

Grill or toast the bread. Rub the garlic over one side of the bread, then brush with 2 tablespoons of the oil. Season with salt and pepper.

Make a vinaigrette dressing with the rest of the oil, the vinegar and a little salt and pepper. Pour it over the tomatoes and let them marinate for 1 hour. Drain.

Spread a layer of ricotta on the bruschetta and cover that with a layer of tomatoes. Sprinkle with basil and adjust the seasoning if necessary before cutting each bruschetta in half. Serve immediately.

Bruschetta

Chopped Chicken Liver and Sage Bruschetta

For 8 bruschetta
4 slices country-style bread
4 tbsp oil, sunflower
or peanut
1 small onion, thinly sliced
1 garlic clove, thinly sliced
200 g/6½ oz chicken liver
2 tbsp sage, chopped
salt, freshly ground pepper
2-3 whole garlic cloves , peeled
8 whole sage leaves

In a frying pan, heat half the oil and cook the onion until it is golden. Add the garlic and then the liver. Cook for 5 minutes being careful not to overcook the liver. Add the chopped sage leaves. Season with salt and pepper.

Purée the liver in a food processor.

Grill or toast the bread. Rub the garlic over one side of the bread, then brush with the rest of the oil.

Spread 1 tablespoon of the liver on each piece of prepared bread. Decorate with the whole sage leaves. Cut each bruschetta in half and serve.

Warm Lentils and Foie Gras Bruschetta ▸

For 10 bruschetta
1 baguette
100 g/3 oz organic lentils
1 bay leaf
1 carrot, sliced
1 tbsp wine vinegar
4 tbsp olive oil
1 chopped shallot
1 tbsp chopped chives
½ foie gras, mi-cuit (partially
preserved)
salt, freshly ground pepper

In a saucepan cover the lentils, carrot and bay leaf with water. Bring to the boil and let cook for 20-25 minutes. Drain well.

Prepare the vinaigrette with the vinegar, olive oil, shallot, and chives. Salt well.

Cut the baguette into 10 slices, ½ inch (1 cm) thick, angles slices. Grill or toast before layering them with lentils and 2 thin slices of foie gras. Season with pepper.

Bruschetta

Sardine Bruschetta

For 12 bruschetta
6 thick slices of country-style bread
2 red peppers, roasted (see p. 141)
4 tbsp pesto (see p. 134)
6 sardines
freshly ground pepper

Preheat oven to 180 °C/350 °F/th. 4.

Cut the peppers into thin strips lengthwise. Spread a generous spoonful of pesto on each slice of bread. Cover with red pepper slices and then carefully arrange filleted sardine halves (center bone removed).

Season with pepper.

Put the bruschetta in the oven 8-10 minutes, but don't let it burn.
Cut each bruschetta in half and serve warm.

Anchovy and Goat's Cheese Bruschetta

For 8 bruschetta
4 slices sourdough bread
8 fresh anchovies, marinated
juice of 1 lemon
100 g/3½ oz rocket
1 tbsp vinegar
4 tbsp olive oil
salt, freshly ground pepper
2 or 3 cloves garlic
200 g/7 oz fresh goat's cheese,
mashed.

Marinate the anchovies in the lemon for 10 minutes.

Mix the rocket with the olive oil, vinegar, salt and pepper.

Grill or toast the bread. Rub the garlic over it and then brush with olive oil.

Spread the cheese on the bruschetta, layer that with an anchovy and top with rocket leaves.

Cut each bruschetta in half and serve.

Bruschetta

Sherry Crab ▸

For 8 open-faced sandwiches
1 baguette, sliced and toasted (optional)
125 g/4 oz cream cheese, softened
250 g/8oz crabmeat
1 tbsp butter
1 shallot, minced
$1/2$ red pepper, chopped
$1/2$ yellow pepper, chopped
1 tbsp sherry
1 tsp thyme
1 pinch Cayenne pepper
1 tbsp chopped chives
juice of $1/2$ lemon
$1/2$ tsp coarse salt

Stir the cream cheese well and fold in the crabmeat. Set aside.

Melt butter in a pan, add shallots and peppers and cook on low heat until tender, 8-10 minutes. Deglaze with sherry and transfer to cream cheese mixture.

Add remaining ingredients and mix well. Serve warm on baguette slices.

Chopped Herring

For 3 open-faced sandwiches
3 slices rye bread
2 hardboiled eggs
2 rollmop herrings
$1/2$ medium onion, chopped
1 small cored apple, quartered but not peeled
20 g/1 oz bread, crust removed
1 tpsp oil
$1/2$ tsp sugar (optional)

Peel the eggs, then separate the white from the yolk.

Drain the rollmops, reserving the liquid and rinse under running water. Place them in a food processor with the onion, apple, boiled egg whites and one of the yolks.

Dip the bread into the herring liquid. Press out excess liquid, then add the bread to the processor, and grind everything up together. Then add the oil and blend until the mixture is very smooth. Taste; if it is too tart or bitter, add a bit of sugar, and possibly more bread.

Crumble the remaining yolk over the sandwiches for decoration before serving.

Marinated Sea Bass

For 6 open-faced sandwiches
6 slices country-style bread
300 g/9 oz sea bass,
cut into very thin slices
juice of 1 lime
1 jalapeño pepper, seeded and
sliced in little rings
3 spring onions, chopped
2 tbsp chopped dill
3 tomatoes
salt, freshly ground pepper
a few drops olive oil

Prepare the marinade: place the fish slices in the lime juice and cover with the jalapeño, onion and dill. Cover with plastic film and marinate for 1 hour in a cool spot.

Cut one of the tomatoes in half and rub it on the bread so that the tomato pulp is absorbed by the bread. Season the bread slices with salt and pepper and a few drops of olive oil.

Cut the other tomatoes into thin slices.

Drain the fish and adjust the seasoning. Place the fish on the bread, alternating with tomato slices. Serve.

Lobster and Avocado

For 2 open-faced sandwiches
2 slices sourdough
or country-style bread
1 avocado, peeled and stoned
1 tsp finely chopped onion
1 tsp fresh lemon juice
salt, freshly ground pepper
a few leaves lamb's lettuce
or mâche
100 g/3½ oz lobster meat, cut in
small chunks

Mash the avocado, and stir in the chopped onion, lemon juice, salt and pepper.

Spoon this purée on the bread, then add a few lettuce leaves or mâche. Layer the lobster meat on top, pressing it lightly into the purée. Serve immediately.

These sandwiches are also good with crayfish or shrimp instead of the lobster. And the bread can be toasted.

Soft-boiled Egg

For 4 open-faced sandwiches
4 slices country-style bread
1 shallot, chopped
500 g/1 lb ripe tomatoes
2 tbsp olive oil
1 star anise
a few thyme sprigs
1 bay leaf
salt, freshly ground pepper
8 large fresh eggs
200 g/6½ oz rocket
sea salt

Peel, seed then cut the tomatoes in cubes . Heat 1 tablespoon of the olive oil in a frying pan, add the shallot and cook over medium heat for 10 minutes, until soft. Add the tomatoes, the anise, thyme, bay leaf, and continue to cook until the liquid has evaporated. Remove the anise and the herbs. Season to taste with salt and pepper. Set aside.

Place the eggs in boiling water for exactly 4 minutes, then plunge them into cold water to stop the cooking process. Keep the boiling water hot under a medium flame.

In another frying pan heat the rest of the oil, and over a low flame, cook the rocket for 2 minutes. Set aside.

Spread the bread slices with the tomato-onion mixture, then pile on a layer of rocket.

Plunge the peeled eggs back into the boiling water for 30 seconds to warm them up, then place them directly on the rocket. Put 2 eggs side by side on each bread slice.

Sprinkle with salt and pepper and serve immediately.

You can replace the rocket with swiss chard, chopped into small pieces and cooked for 5-7 minutes.

Open-faced Sandwiches

Chopped Chicken Liver

For 3 open-faced sandwiches
3 slices rye bread
100 g/3½ oz chicken livers
1 tbsp chicken fat
1 onion, thinly sliced
1 hardboiled egg
salt, freshly ground pepper
a few pickles

In a heavy-bottomed frying pan, sauté the livers in the chicken fat. When they are pink, remove from heat to a dish; do not overcook them.

Fry the onions in the same fat, or add some more if necessary, and cook until tender. In a food processor, blend them with the egg and the liver. Add salt and pepper to taste.

Grill the bread, and spoon on the liver mixture. The bread can be cut into 2 or more pieces. Serve with pickles.

You can add chopped celery leaves or lovage to the above mixture for a delicious variation.

Cèpes

For 8 open-faced sandwiches
8 slices country-style bread,
5 inches diameter
800 g/1½ lb cèpes (or porcini)
salt, freshly ground pepper
4 tbsp olive oil
2 garlic cloves

Preheat the over to 220 °C/400 °F/th. 6.

Wash the cèpes or porcini carefully, remove the stems, only keeping the caps. Season the under part of the caps with salt and pepper and dribble lightly with 2 tablespoons of the olive oil. Place the mushrooms on a baking sheet and cook until they are nicely grilled.

Pour some of the rest of the olive oil into a frying pan and heat over a medium flame. Fry the bread slices golden brown, adding more oil when necessary.

Rub the bread with the garlic and place the mushroom caps, inside down, on the bread. Serve warm.

Onion Fondue with Olives

For 8 open-faced sandwiches
8 slices sourdough bread, grilled
1 kg/2 lb large, sweet onions
4 tbsp olive oil
2 tbsp anchovy paste
1 handful fresh thyme
(or 2 tsp dried)
4 tbsp black olives, pitted
and drained
salt, freshly ground pepper
3 tbsp tapenade (see p. 130)
3 tbsp chopped basil

Peel the onions and mince them in a food processor.

In a frying pan with 1 tablespoon of oil, heat the anchovy paste until it liquifies, then add the onions, thyme and the rest of the oil.

Cook on low heat for 40 minutes, until the onions are almost a purée. Remove from heat and fold in the olives. Add salt and pepper to taste, but be careful not to add too much salt, as other ingredients are salty.

Spread the bread with tapenade, then spoon on the onion preparation. Top with the basil before serving.

Open-faced Sandwiches

Fig and Brie ▸

For 2 open-faced sandwiches
2 whole-wheat or rye
Swedish crackers
1 tbsp butter
2 leaves red trevise lettuce
6 thin slices of Brie cheese,
rind removed
2 fresh figs cut in quarters
juice of 1 lime

Butter the crackers, then place a leaf of trevise on each. Arrange the Brie slices on top, pressing lightly.

Sprinkle the figs with lime juice, and then delicately place them on the Brie. Serve.

Goat's Cheese and Raisin

For 4 open-faced sandwichs
4 slices country-style white bread, toasted
2 tbsp homemade ketchup
(see p. 136)
80-100 g/3 oz fresh goat's cheese
a handful raisins
freshly ground pepper

Preheat the over to 180 ℃/350 °F/th. 4.

Spread the ketchup on the bread slices. Slice the cheese carefully with a sharp knife, and place the slices on the bread. Sprinkle the raisins over this, and season with pepper.

Heat in the oven 5 minutes (cover with tin foil to keep the raisins from burning), or in a microwave for 90 seconds. Serve hot.

‹ Goat's Cheese and Pear

For 4 open-faced sandwiches
4 slices sourdough bread, grilled
80-100 g/3 oz fresh goat's cheese
1 ripe pear, peeled and thinly sliced
a handful pine nuts
a handful raisins
freshly ground pepper

Preheat the over to 180 ℃/350 °F/th. 4.

Spread the cheese on the bread then place the pear slices on top. Sprinkle with pine nuts and raisins, and season with pepper.

Heat in the oven 5 minutes, or in a microwave for 90 seconds. Serve hot.

You can poach the pear in spiced red wine before cutting into thin slices.

Époisses Cheese and Tomato

For 4 open-faced sandwiches
4 slices sourdough bread, lightly grilled
8 slices tomato, peeled
8 slices Époisses cheese
4 thin slices onion
freshly ground pepper

Preheat the over to 180 ℃/350 °F/th. 4.

Keep the cheese in the refrigerator until ready to use to make it easier to slice. Place the tomato slices on the bread, then the cheese and onion. Season with pepper. Heat in the oven for 5 minutes, or in a microwave 60-90 seconds. Serve hot.

Leftover Delights

LEFTOVERS are by their very nature approximate and variable. That's why we love them and can concoct all kinds of innovations and happy marriages. They can go a long way by adding an egg, another slice of ham, a few more spoonfuls of chutney, or Chinese mustard, etc. when friends pop by unexpectedly.

Roast Beef ▸

For 1 sandwich
2 slices rye bread, toasted (optional)
½ tsp horseradish
2 thin slices cold roast beef
3 onion slices (optional)
salt, freshly ground pepper
a few pickles

Spread the horseradish on the bread. Place the roast beef on one slice of bread. (Add the onion slices if desired). Season with salt and pepper before closing the sandwich. Cut in half and serve with a few pickles on the side.

You can replace the horseradish by the same quantity of green peppercorn mustard.

Leftover Delights

Cooked Beef

For 1 sandwich
2 slices rye bread,
toasted (optional)
1 tsp mayonnaise (see p. 138)
1 thin slice cooked beef or a few
pieces of pulled-apart stewed meat
1 tbsp ketchup (see p. 136),
mustard, or courgette relish,
(see p. 141)
salt, freshly ground pepper

Spread the mayonnaise on the bread. Place the meat on one slice and add the ketchup, mustard or relish on the other slice. Season with salt and pepper.

Close the sandwich and cut in half.

Braised, stewed or boiled beef make delicious sandwiches for the following day.

‹ Meatloaf

For 1 sandwich
2 slices rye bread
1 tbsp mayonnaise (see p. 138)
1 thick slice meatloaf
1 tbsp homemade ketchup
(see p. 136) or another condiment
salt, freshly ground pepper
FOR THE MEATLOAF:
(about 10 slices per loaf)
3 eggs
3 tbsp breadcrumbs
$1/2$ tsp baking powder
$1^1/2$ tbsp oil, sunflower
or peanut
1 tbsp onion, chopped
1 green pepper, chopped
750 g/$1^1/2$ lb lean ground beef
250 g/8 oz lean ground pork
5 basil leaves, finely chopped
1 handful parsley, chopped

Prepare the meatloaf. Preheat the oven to 150-170 °C/300-325 °F/th. 2-3.

Beat the eggs and add the breadcrumbs and the baking powder and set aside.

In a frying pan, heat 1 tablespoon of the oil, and when hot, add the onion and pepper. Cook the vegetables for about 5 minutes. Incorporate the meat into the egg mixture and then add the vegetables, herbs, salt and pepper. Mix well.

Form a loaf and put it into an oiled dish (the other $1/2$ tablespoon) then bake in the oven for about 1 hour. Be careful the meat doesn't dry out.

Prepare the sandwich. Spread the mayonnaise on the bread. Place the meatloaf on one slice. Spread ketchup or another condiment on the other slice, salt and pepper. Close the sandwich and cut in half before serving.

Leftover cold meatloaf is a true delight on a rye bread sandwich. It's worth making the meatloaf just for leftovers!

Turkey and Apple Mustard

For 1 sandwich
2 slices rye bread or pumpernickel
100-150 g/3-5 oz cold
cooked turkey
2 tbsp apple mustard (see p. 135)
salt, freshly ground pepper

Cut the turkey into thin slices. Spread the apple mustard on the bread and place the turkey on one slice. Season the meat with salt and pepper before closing the sandwich. Cut in half and serve immediately.

Leftover Delights

Duck Breast with Homemade Pickles

For two open-faced sandwiches
2 slices sourdough bread, toasted
1 tsp mustard
3 tbsp homemade pickles
(see p. 138)
6-8 thin slices duck breast
salt, freshly ground pepper

Spread a fine layer of mustard and then pickles on the bread.
Place the duck on the bread. Season to taste with salt and pepper. Serve immediately.

You can replace the pickles by courgette relish (see p. 141).

Minced Ham

For 2 sandwiches
2 individual ciabattas
2 tbsp onion, chopped
2 tbsp homemade ketchup
(see p. 136)
2 tbsp green pepper, chopped
2 tbsp pickles, chopped
100 g/3 oz hard cheese (mimolette, cheddar, etc.), grated
100 g/3 oz minced ham
salt, freshly ground pepper

Mix all the ingredients together in a big bowl. Make sure the seasoning is right. Fill the ciabattas with the preparation and serve immediately.

Omelette or Scrambled Eggs ▸

For 1 sandwich
2 slices sourdough or white bread, toasted
15 g/½ oz butter
1 tbsp ketchup (see p. 136), tomato chutney (see p. 132), or courgette relish (see p. 141)
leftover omelette or scrambled eggs
salt, freshly ground pepper

Butter the 2 slices of bread. Spread your chosen condiment on them.
Place the eggs on 1 of the slices and season them.

Close the sandwich with the other slice. Cut in half and serve.

Cold Fish with Horseradish and Capers

For 4 sandwiches
4 individual pitas
300 g/10 oz cold cooked fish
4 tbsp celery or
lovage leaves, chopped
1 tbsp horseradish
2 tbsp capers
salt, freshly ground pepper
2 tbsp mayonnaise (see p. 138)

Mash the fish with a fork and incorporate the celery, horseradish and capers. Add salt, pepper and mix again. Adjust the seasoning if necessary. Open the pitas and spread the mayonnaise. Divide the fish preparation among the pitas and serve immediately.

Cold Fish with Peppers

For 4 sandwiches
4 individual ciabattas
½ green pepper cut, thinly sliced
½ red, orange, or yellow pepper, thinly sliced
2 spring onions, thinly sliced
1 tbsp olive oil
300 g/10 oz cold cooked fish
2 tbsp mayonnaise (see p. 138)
juice of 1 lemon
5 tbsp parsley, chopped
sea salt with herbs and spices
freshly ground pepper
2 tbsp butter

Lightly fry the onions and peppers in the olive oil until tender. Mash the fish with a fork and incorporate the mayonnaise, lemon juice and parsley. Add salt, pepper and mix well. Adjust the seasoning if necessary.

Open the ciabattas and butter the insides. Distribute the fish mixture among the ciabattas and then add the pepper-onion mixture on top. Cover and serve immediately.

Cold Fish with Relish

For 5 open-faced sandwiches
5 slices pumpernickel, toasted
300 g/10 oz cold cooked fish
5 tbsp dill, chopped
3-4 tbsp courgette relish (see p. 141)
2 spring onions, thinly sliced
freshly ground pepper

Mash the fish with a fork and add the dill, relish and onion. Season with pepper, mix well and adjust seasoning if necessary.

Spread the mixture on the bread and serve immediately.

You can replace the relish by the same quantity of tomato chutney, (see p. 132).

Sandwich Spreads and Trimmings

The **SPREADS AND TRIMMINGS** in this chapter will come in handy at party time particularly. Serve generous portions on thin slices of toasted white or sourdough bread, crackers or crisp bread.

Or why not serve them in pretty bowls next to a breadbasket brimming with many varieties of bread and let your guests compose their own sandwiches?

Blue Cheese and Spring Onion ▸

For 4 open-faced sandwiches
125 g/4 oz blue cheese
75 g/3½ oz cream cheese
3 tbsp double cream, crème fraîche
or thick yoghurt
1 onion, finely chopped
½ tsp curry powder
salt, freshly ground pepper

Mash the cheese with a fork. Put the cream or yoghurt into a strainer and drain for at least 1 hour. Then add it along with the onion to the blue cheese and cream cheese. Mix in the curry and adjust the seasoning. Spread this mixture on the bread of your choice and serve immediately.

Sandwich Spreads

Thick Yoghurt and Fresh Herbs

For 4-6 open-faced sandwiches
200 g/6-7 oz thick yoghurt or
ricotta cheese
100 g/3 oz fresh goat's cheese
1 garlic clove, chopped
1 pinch Cayenne pepper
salt, freshly ground pepper
1 handful mixed chopped herbs
(lovage, oregano, basil, tarragon,
chives, chervil, etc.)

Put the yoghurt or ricotta into a strainer and drain for at least 1 hour. Mix the cheese and yoghurt or ricotta together. Add the well-chopped herbs. Season with salt and pepper, and adjust the seasoning, if necessary. Spread a generous spoonful of this preparation on the bread of your choice and serve immediately.

Caponata

For 20-30 canapés
2 tbsp capers
8 anchovy fillets
3-4 tbsp olive oil
1 aubergine (500 g/$\frac{1}{2}$ lb), cubed
$\frac{1}{2}$ medium red pepper, cubed
$\frac{1}{2}$ medium green pepper, cubed
1 medium onion, chopped
2 tbsp garlic, chopped
1 tbsp brown sugar
50 cl/16 fl oz red wine vinegar
125 ml/4 fl oz tomato purée
1 handful basil leaves, chopped
salt, freshly ground pepper

Chop half of the capers and set them aside.

Cut the anchovies into pieces and set aside.

In half the oil, sauté the aubergine for 10-15 minutes, or until very tender. Set aside.

In the rest of the oil, sauté the peppers for the same amount of time until they're very well cooked. Set aside. Add, if necessary, a bit more oil then sauté the onion and garlic. Add the sugar and vinegar and cook for a few minutes before adding the tomato purée and the chopped capers.

Let the mixture cook on a low flame for 15 minutes, until the sauce thickens.

Pour the tomato preparation over the other vegetables; add the whole capers, anchovies and herbs.

Mix well and season if necessary. Spread a generous amount of this preparation on the bread of your choice and serve immediately.

◂ Salsa Sauce

For about 20 canapés
2 tomatoes, chopped
1 medium red pepper, finely chopped
1 medium onion, chopped
$\frac{1}{2}$ tsp jalapeño pepper cut in very thin strips
1 big handful fresh coriander, chopped
salt, freshly ground pepper

Put all the ingredients in a bowl for at least 20 minutes. Spread the mixture on little canapés or sandwiches and serve immediately. Adjust the amount of jalapeño pepper to your taste. It is very hot.

Sandwich Spreads

Aubergine Caviar

For about 20 canapés
1 aubergine (500 g/½ lb)
1 tsp chopped garlic
1 small onion, chopped
3 tbsp chopped parsley
salt, freshly ground pepper
1 tbsp olive oil
juice of 1 lemon
a few black olives

Cook the whole aubergine in a preheated over, 180 °C/350 °F/th. 4, for 20-25 minutes (or in a microwave for 7 minutes, at maximum power) until the skin blackens and the flesh is soft.

Remove the flesh and put it in a strainer to remove as much liquid as possible. In a food processor, make a purée of the aubergine, garlic, onion, and parsley. Season with salt and pepper, then add the oil and the lemon juice. Adjust the seasoning by adding more lemon juice and salt if necessary.

This caviar can be kept in the refrigerator for up to 5 days. Serve it on the bread of your choice, and decorate with a few black olives.

Sandwich spreads

Guacamole

For about 30 canapés
2 avocados
1 tomato, peeled, cored and chopped
1 tbsp onion (or scallion),
finely chopped
1 garlic clove, chopped
$^{1}/_{2}$ tsp chili powder
2 tsp chopped coriander
1 tbsp lemon juice
salt, freshly ground pepper

Mash the avocado with a fork. Incorporate the other ingredients. Mix well and adjust the seasoning, if necessary. Prepare the guacamole as close to serving time as possible.

Serve it spread on little canapés.

Hummus

For about 20 canapés
425 g/14 oz chick peas, canned
3 garlic cloves
25 cl/8 fl oz tahina
juice of 2 lemons
a few drops Tabasco
salt
3 tbsp olive oil

In a food processor, purée the chick peas, their juice, the garlic cloves and the tahina. Add the lemon juice, the Tabasco, olive oil and salt. Mix again. The purée should be thick and smooth. Adjust the seasoning, adding more lemon juice and salt, if necessary.

Serve immediately spread on little canapés.

The condiments in this chapter – chutneys, pesto, mayonnaise, ketchup, etc. – are precious additions for delicious and original sandwiches.

Anchovy Paste ▸

For 1 jar 25 cl/8 oz/1 cup
200 g/6½ oz anchovies
2 garlic cloves, chopped
freshly ground pepper
½ tsp vinegar
15 cl/4½ fl oz olive oil

Fillet each anchovy. Rinse well.

In a mortar, pound the anchovies with the garlic, pepper and vinegar. Pour in the oil very slowly, like you would for mayonnaise, making a smooth paste. This can also be prepared in a food processor.

Anchovy paste will keep very well in the refrigerator for 1 month, covered with a film of olive oil.

Tapenade

For 1 jar 45 cl/15 oz/2 cups
300 black Provençal olives, pitted
1 garlic clove, peeled
1 handful parsley
4 anchovy fillets
2 tbsp olive oil

Purée the olives, garlic, parsley and anchovies in a food processor.

Incorporate the oil to get a smooth purée.

Tapenade keeps for at least 2 weeks in the refrigerator.

Garlic Purée

For 1 jar 20 cl/7 oz/scant 1 cup
1 head garlic
1 tbsp olive oil

Heat the oven to 160 °C/325 °F/th. 3.

Separate the cloves without peeling them and place on a sheet of aluminium foil. Pour the oil over them and then wrap them in the foil, making a *papillote*. Bake for 40-50 min.

Squeeze the cloves into a bowl, removing the envelope.

This purée can keep in the refrigerator for 2-3 weeks in a little tightly closed jar.

Trimmings

Tomato Chutney

For 4 jars 50 cl/16 fl oz/2 cups
1 kg/2 lb ripe tomatoes
1 branch celery
1 small red pepper
1 small green pepper
400 g/13 oz onions
1 kg/2 lb sour apples
40 cl/13½ fl oz/scant 2 cups cider vinegar
100 g/3½ oz/½ cup sugar
1 tbsp pickling salt
170 g/5½ oz raisins

Blanch the tomatoes for 10 seconds in boiling water, then remove their skins. Set aside.

Chop the celery, peppers, and onions. Peel and core the apples and cut them in small pieces.

Put the apples and vegetables in a saucepan with the vinegar, sugar and salt. Bring to the boil and then lower the flame and let it simmer. Stir regularly so it doesn't stick.

Continue cooking until much of the liquid has evaporated and the chutney looks transparent. Once it has reduced, add the raisins. Let it cook for 20 more minutes, stirring all the time.

Spoon into clean jars and close tightly. Chutney keeps for a few years in a cool place.

Tomato Ginger Chutney ▸

For 4 jars 50 cl/16 fl oz/2 cups
2 kg/4½ lb ripe tomatoes
150 g/5 oz candied ginger
6 garlic cloves, peeled
25 cl/8 fl oz/1 cup cider vinegar
150 g/5 oz raisins
200 g/6½ oz/1 cup brown sugar
2 tbsp salt
½ tbsp Szechuan pepper

Blanch the tomatoes for 10 seconds in boiling water, then remove their skins. When cool, cut them into pieces.

Chop the ginger and garlic.

In a saucepan, bring the vinegar to the boil and add all the other ingredients. Lower the flame and let it simmer for 1½ hours, until the sauce reduces and thickens, stirring regularly to prevent it from sticking.

Spoon the preparation into clean jars and close tightly. Chutney keeps for a few years in a cool place.

Trimmings

Pesto

For 1 jar of 25 cl/8 fl oz/1 cup
2 handfuls basil (about 100 g/3¹/₂ oz)
3 tbsp pine nuts
1 big garlic clove, peeled
3 tbsp grated Parmesan cheese
8-10 cl/3 fl oz/¹/₃ cup olive oil
salt, freshly ground pepper

Mix together all the ingredients in a food processor for 20 seconds to get a smooth, thick sauce. Adjust the seasoning, if necessary.

Spoon the mixture into a clean jar and close tightly.

Pesto keeps for at least 2 weeks in the refrigerator.

Basil Coulis

For 1 jar of 25 cl/8 fl oz/1 cup
2 handfuls basil
(about 100 g/3¹/₂ oz)
1 garlic clove, peeled
25 cl/8 fl oz/1 cup olive oil

Blend the basil and garlic together in a food processor. Cover with the olive oil and then mix well to get a smooth purée.

Pour the mixture into a clean jar and close tightly. Basil coulis will keep for several weeks in the refrigerator.

Trimmings

Apple Mustard

For 1 jar 45 cl/13½ fl oz/2 cups
1 tbsp Dijon mustard
2 tbsp olive oil
250 g/8 oz peeled acid apples,
cored and cut into pieces
1 tsp paprika
½ tsp salt
juice of ½ lemon
2 tsp cider vinegar

Mix the mustard togetherwith the oil in a food processor then add the other ingredients. The sauce should be thick and smooth. Taste and adjust the seasoning.

Spoon the mixture into a clean jar and close tightly. Apple mustard will keep for several weeks in the refrigerator.

Chinese Mustard

For 1 jar 45 cl/13½ fl oz/2 cups
juice of 1 lemon
1 tbsp Dijon mustard
6 cl/2 fl oz/¼ cup white
wine vinegar
a few drops of soy sauce
2 anchovy fillets
2 garlic cloves, peeled
2 egg yolks
25 cl/8 fl oz/1 cup olive oil

In a food processor mix together the lemon juice, mustard, vinegar, soy sauce, anchovies, garlic and egg yolks. Incorporate the oil very gradually until you achieve the consistency of mayonnaise.

Pour the mixture into a clean jar and close tightly. Chinese mustard will keep for several months in the refrigerator.

Ketchup

For 3 jars 25 cl/8 fl oz/1 cup
2 kg/2½ lb ripe tomatoes
4 garlic cloves
1 onion
1 red or green pepper
1 tsp peppercorns
15 allspice berries
10 cloves
10 cl/3½ fl oz/scant ½ cup cider vinegar
50 g/2 oz brown sugar
½ stick cinnamon
4 tsp salt
1 tsp celery seeds
2 tsp paprika
1 large pinch Cayenne pepper

Peel the tomatoes after plunging them in boiling water for 10 seconds. Cut them up and cook for 10-15 minutes over a medium heat. (You can drain and save the tomato water to make soup.)

In a big saucepan, chop the garlic, onion, and pepper. Add the chopped tomatoes and cook the mixture over a medium heat until it reduces considerably.

Put the peppercorns and cloves in a tea ball or a piece of cheesecloth and add to the mixture.

Incorporate the vinegar, brown sugar, cinnamon, salt, celery seed, paprika and Cayenne pepper. Stir well and continue reducing it for about 1 hour over a gentle heat. Stir. When the sauce has thickened, remove the tea ball or cheesecloth and the cinnamon stick, wait for it to cool down then purée it. Return it to a gentle heat, stirring constantly, and let it continue to thicken. Adjust the seasoning, if necessary, then pour the ketchup into clean jars. Close them tightly. Ketchup will keep for several years in a cool place.

Chili Ketchup ▸

For 1 jar of 25 cl/8 fl oz/1 cup
200 g/6½ oz thick yoghurt or sour cream
1 tbsp homemade ketchup (see above)
1 tbsp chili powder
1 onion, chopped
1 tbsp Worcestershire sauce
1 tbsp chopped chives
salt, freshly ground pepper

Purée all the ingredients in a food processor into a smooth sauce. You can keep this chili ketchup for a week in the refrigerator, covered.

Chili powder varies greatly in strength. Adjust the quantity to your taste.

Trimmings

Mayonnaise ▸

For 1 jar 300 g/9 oz
2 egg yolks
½ tsp Dijon mustard
1 pinch salt
1 pinch white pepper
25 cl/8 fl oz sunflower
or peanut oil
2 tbsp lemon juice

All the ingredients should be at room temperature. Place the yolks, mustard, salt and pepper in a food processor. Add a tablespoon of the oil and mix. Continue to blend while pouring in a thin stream of oil. Just before all the oil has been added, incorporate the lemon juice, then add the rest of the oil. Adjust the seasoning.

Mayonnaise will keep for several days in the refrigerator in a tightly closed jar.

Homemade Pickles

For 4 jars 50 cl/16 fl oz/2 cups
1½ kg/3 lb cucumbers
250 g/8 oz onions
4 tbsp pickling salt
100 g/3½ oz brown sugar
1 tsp turmeric
1 tsp ground ginger
1 pinch red pepper
1 tbsp cornstarch
4 tbsp Dijon mustard
40 cl/12 fl oz/scant 2 cups cider vinegar
12 cl/4 fl oz/½ cup water

Cut the cucumbers and onions in thin slices. Put them in a bowl and distribute the pickling salt over them. Put aside for at least 3 hours or overnight. Then rinse and drain.

In a big saucepan, add the sugar, spices, cornstarch, mustard, vinegar and water. Cover and bring to the boil. Add the drained cucumbers and onions, bring to the boil again and remove from the heat.

Distribute the vegetables in the prepared jars and close them tightly. These pickles will keep for several years in a cool place.

Make homemade pickles from your own seasonal vegetables or from those bought at markets when prices are at their lowest and produce at its best. The basic idea is to preserve vegetables in brine, made from vinegar and salt, with varying quantities and types of spices and sugar.

Trimmings

Courgette Relish

For 3 jars of 50 cl/16 fl oz/2 cups
1 tbsp pickling salt
1 kg/2 lb courgettes, grated
250 g/½ lb onions, chopped
12½ cl/4 fl oz/½ cup cider vinegar
50 g/2 oz/½ cup brown sugar
1 tbsp curcuma
2 tsp nutmeg
1 tbsp dry mustard
½ green pepper, chopped
½ red pepper, chopped

In a big bowl, sprinkle the pickling salt over the courgettes and onions and leave for at least 12 hours. Rinse and drain.

In a saucepan, mix together the vinegar, brown sugar and spices.

Bring to the boil, add all the vegetables and let boil for 15 minutes.

Pour the hot relish into the prepared jars. Close tightly. The relish will keep for at least a year in a cool place.

◄ Roasted Peppers

For 2 peppers
1 tbsp olive oil

Heat the grill or oven to 200 °C/400 °F/th. 6.

Place the whole peppers in the oven or under the grill. Let them cook until their skin blisters, about 15 minutes.

Put them into a bowl covered with cling wrap. When cool, remove the skin and seeds and cut them in strips.

To preserve them, spread with olive oil before putting in a tightly closed container in the refrigerator. They'll keep for a few weeks.

You can also prepare them in the microwave. Cook at maximum power for 3 minutes. Adjust the time for your oven. Wrap them in a plastic bag and let cool. Proceed as above.

Trimmings

Index